Text: Natasha Edwards
Photography: Caroline Jones
Managing Editor: Clare Peel
Series Editor: Tony Halliday

Berlitz POCKET GUIDE

Lille

First Edition 2005
Updated 2006

PHOTOGRAPHY
By Caroline Jones except page 41, by Lauros/Giraudon/AKG.
Cover photograph: David Hughes/Robert Harding Picture Library.

CONTACTING THE EDITORS

Every effort has been made to provide accurate information in this publication, but changes are inevitable. The publisher cannot be responsible for any resulting loss, inconvenience or injury. We would appreciate it if readers would call our attention to any errors or outdated information by contacting Berlitz Publishing, PO Box 7910, London SE1 1WE, England. Fax: (44) 20 7403 0290; e-mail: berlitz@apaguide.co.uk www.berlitzpublishing.com

Printed in Singapore by Insight Print Services (Pte) Ltd, 38 Joo Koon Road, Singapore 628990.
Tel: (65) 6865-1600. Fax: (65) 6861-6438

Berlitz Trademark Reg. U.S. Patent Office and other countries. Marca Registrada

Works by Goya, Brueghel, Rodin and Rubens feature at the excellent Palais des Beaux-Arts (page 45)

The Musée de l'Hospice Comtesse (page 32), an intimate museum in an historic hospice

A typical Flemish *hallekerke,* the Eglise St-Maurice (page 39) is Lille's finest church

TOP TEN ATTRACTIONS

Flamboyant legacy of Louis XIV: the Porte de Paris (page 41)

Kids will love the driverless VAL Métro trains (page 95). Some stations are impressive too, such as the Lille Europe Métro, decorated with murals

The 17th-century Vieille Bourse (page 27), set in the medieval market square of the Grand' Place, is a magnificent reminder of Lille's glorious Flemish past

A lively market (page 50) takes over central Wazemmes on Sunday

A museum in a swimming pool: Roubaix's La Piscine (page 60)

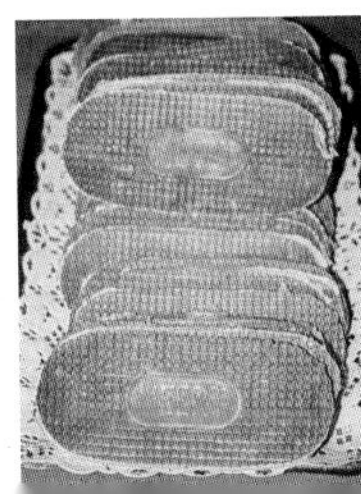

Try delicious waffles at Pâtisserie Méert (page 30), a Lille landmark

The Maison Folie de Wazemmes (page 50) is among a dozen disused buildings given new leases of life as cultural centres

CONTENTS

Fact Sheets

INTRODUCTION

Lille is a proudly northern French city, not just in its architecture, but also its cuisine, folklore and sense of hospitality. If, for many French people, Lille still conjures up images of industrial gloom and declining textile industries, then one look at the richly decorated Flemish houses, the elegant *hôtels particuliers* (private mansions) and fanciful villas gives some idea of how wealthy Lille was in the past. And the city is also going through a revival. Its position at an international crossroads between France, Belgium and Great Britain, good transport links and role as regional capital, boosted by the prestige of being European City of Culture in 2004, have all contributed to a new confidence, the rediscovery of its cultural riches and renovation of its architectural heritage. However, what makes Lille most distinctive is its blend of French and Flemish. Long a prize in battles between France and Flanders, the city's identity is a unique combination of the two.

The Lillois

With 220,000 inhabitants, Lille is only France's tenth-largest city; however, it is the centre of Lille Métropole, a metropolis of 1.1 million inhabitants, the fourth-largest conurbation in France and the heart of one of the smallest but most densely populated French regions. It is also the youngest: 41 percent of the population is under 25. Add to this a large student community – over 90,000 students, divided between the Université de Lille (one of the biggest in France), based in Lille and Villeneuve d'Ascq, the Université Catholique in the Vauban area, the Institut des Sciences-Politiques, Roubaix's ESMOD fashion design school and France's most respected journalism school.

Elaborate architecture in Vieux Lille

As well as being the word used by *nordistes* to describe themselves, *Ch'ti* is also the name they give to the local dialect. Linguists view it as a form of old French, close to Picard, although a few Flemish words have crept in too. Once largely reserved for the peasants and working classes, there are now *Ch'ti* songs, radio broadcasts and theatre productions, and it has become trendy to be able to drop a few words into the conversation. *Quo qu'te bos?* (What are you drinking?) might do the trick.

Contemporary Lille is a lively multicultural city, the result of waves of immigration to work in the region's mines and textile factories. Belgians and Italians in the 19th century and Poles during the early 20th century have been succeeded by immigrants from France's former colonies in the Maghreb and West Africa.

Festivals and Traditions

The *Ch'timi*, or *Ch'ti*, as the northerners are called, are renowned for their hospitality and love of festivities. Tourists will often find a genuine welcome here that is not always apparent in hectic Paris, the reputedly snooty Côte d'Azur or other more touristy parts of France, along with a calendar of lovingly preserved pastimes and festivities.

If you travel much around the area, you are almost certain to come across a parade of giants. The centuries-old tradition grew out of religious parades illustrating Biblical stories in the Middle Ages to become secular festivities; giants, costumed figures made out of wood and wicker, often illustrating local trades or some supposedly heroic moment in local history, are paraded around the town at the head of a noisy procession (Gayant in Douai, Reuze Papa and Reuze Maman in Cassel, Gargantua in Bailleul, Goliath and his wife at Ath, Phinaert and Lydéric in Lille, *see page 13*). Then there are other celebrations, from herring throwing in Dunkerque during *Carnaval* or the little cakes thrown from the balcony of the town hall in Armentières to the arrival of St Nicolas before Christmas and the colossal street market that is the Grande Braderie de Lille each September *(see page 93)*.

A resurgence of interest in local culture can be seen in the comeback of the *Ch'ti* dialect *(see box)* in *estaminets* – the typically northern form of convivial bar, serving beer and regional dishes and where you can often play traditional games such as skittles, billiards, crochets (rings thrown on to hooks on a target) and *toptafel* (a table for spinning tops). Other local pastimes include *bourles* (a sort of bowls), archery, pigeon racing and, even these days, bloodthirsty cock fighting.

Wazemmes market

Lille for Tourists

Lille as a tourist destination is a fairly recent phenomenon, brought about to a large extent by the arrival of the Eurostar between France and Britain. The discovery of the intimate Flemish architecture of Vieux Lille, of colourful Wazemmes market and upmarket shopping by cross-Channel visitors has encouraged the French, too, to look again at the capital of northern France. Other factors have been the renovation of the Palais de Beaux-Arts and the opening of the superb La Piscine, Musée d'Art et d'Industrie in Roubaix (to be complemented in future by the extension to the Musée d'Art Moderne at Villeneuve d'Ascq). But there is more to see than world-class art; rehabilitated factories are making the most of the city's industrial heritage, while lively bars and great eating opportunities are an equal draw.

Distinguished Heritage

One of the most marked features of Lille's architecture is its use of warm, deep-red brick, combined with the golden stone bands and cornices that are so characteristic of the city's lovely Renaissance and baroque buildings. The houses of poorer families were generally made of wood, until the practice was banned because of fire risk, and only the

Mad as Houses

One of the most exciting aspects of Lille as European City of Culture in 2004 was the creation of 12 Maisons Folies (taking their name from house and folly), intended to be left as a legacy of the prestigious year. The buildings are located not just in the Lille conurbation, but across the area, including in Arras and Mauberge, and over the border at Courtrai and Tournai. They reflect different aspects of the area's past, ranging from a brewery, textile factory and farm to fortresses and an 18th-century mansion. Their new uses include artists' studios, music rehearsal rooms, performance spaces, cafés and galleries, as well as the more unexpected: a hammam at the Maison Folie de Wazemmes and an experimental garden on the roof of the Condition Publique. The architectural solutions are widely different, too, from the minimalist renovation of the Fort de Mons and historically respectful Hospice de Havre at Tourcoing to the experimental cloud-like organic mesh of steel floating over Wazemmes by Dutch architect Lars Spuybroek and NOX.

wealthiest used stone. A distinctively Flemish style grew up, with tall, narrow, gabled façades – sometimes hiding surprisingly large premises behind – and ornate, deeply carved, sculpted decoration, in contrast to the flatter surface motifs of the so-called French Renaissance seen in the 1572 Hôtel de Beaurepaire (now restaurant La Compostelle). Some of the earlier examples (as seen on place Louise de Bettignies and rue de la Barre) have little decoration and stepped gables known in French as *pas de moine* (monk's footsteps).

Gables, place Louise de Bettignies

Later, the fashion was for cartouches, broken pediments and motifs such as carved dolphins, swags of fruit and cornucopia – a style that reached its peak in the Vieille Bourse in the 1650s. Louis XIV's conquest of the town brought in the desire to stamp the mark of the French monarchy in a more pompous official baroque of the Porte de Paris, but also to lay down architectural rules in the Rang de Beauregard or the Quartier Royale, while the church also wanted to assert its power, as in the weightily domed church of Ste-Marie-Madeleine.

In the 18th century, the nobility built their own fine residences, notably along rue Royale, following the Paris fashion, with the main building hidden at the back of a grand entrance courtyard. During the 19th century, a distinctive type of workers' housing, the cours, went up; these were long terraces of one-up-one-down houses, built around a narrow central courtyard, where there was a communal washhouse. A few examples can still be seen in the Moulins district of Lille and in Roubaix.

In the late 19th and early 20th century, historical revival and eclecticism dominated. Here, this was marked by a neo-Flemish revival, seen in streets such as boulevard Jean-Baptiste Lebas in Lille, boulevard du Général de Gaulle in Roubaix and, at its most exotic, along avenue de l'Hippodrome in Lambersart. Chunky houses in brick with stone facing, coloured tiles, turrets and elaborate gables all made their way into the equation. The interwar rebuilding of the 1920s and 1930s saw another great building period, with art deco apartments and brasseries along rue de Béthune, as well as the lovely Huîtrière restaurant, and the avant-garde Villa Cavois at Croix, designed by Robert Mallet-Stevens.

The Maison Folie de Wazemmes

More recently, Lille has been at the forefront of a far-sighted rehabilitation of former industrial buildings – examples include the pioneering Archives du Monde du Travail in Roubaix and the more recent Condition Publique among the Maisons Folies. Daring modern architectural projects have included the Musée d'Art Moderne at Villeneuve d'Ascq, the minimalist extension to the Palais des Beaux-Arts and the creation in the 1990s of the Euralille quarter, bringing in renowned architects such as Rem Koolhaas and Christian de Portzamparc in a project set to continue into the next decade.

A BRIEF HISTORY

Lille has a dual history: on the one hand, as a prosperous trading and manufacturing centre that was constantly outgrowing its walls; on the other, as a frontier town forever changing hands. One affected the other, as the city's wealth made it an enviable prize and the subject of numerous sieges in the battle for control of the northern plain.

Marshy Beginnings

Lille did indeed begin as L'Isle (the island), a small community somewhere on an island in the River Deûle. In fact the early days of Lille are pretty obscure. There are odd traces of Neolithic and Bronze Age man, Roman tiles and pottery, but no notable settlements in the marshy territory then occupied by various Gaulish tribes. During the Dark Ages, the weakness of the monarchy saw the rise of powerful local counts, better able to protect the local population. Villages grew up at Fins (site of the Eglise St-Maurice at least as far back as

Lydéric and Phinaert

The wicked, bearded giant Phinaert and handsome young hero Lydéric, sculpted at the base of the belfry of the Hôtel de Ville *(see page 41 and photograph on page 1)*, tell the story of the city's creation. According to legend, in 620, bandit lord Phinaert ambushed and slaughtered Burgundian prince Salvaert. Salvaert's beautiful wife Ermengaert escaped and, following an apparition by the Virgin, gave birth to a son, Lydéric. Ermengaert was imprisoned, but Lydéric was brought up in the forest by a hermit. When he was 20, he avenged his father in a duel with Phinaert and was rewarded by King Dagobert with the castle of Buc (present-day Lille) and title of Prince of Flanders.

the 9th century), at Wasemia (Wazemmes) and Ulma (Lomme); however, the first written mention of Lille itself dates only from 1066, when a charter was issued by Baudoin V, Count of Flanders, for the foundation of the Collégiale St-Pierre, where a miracle-making statue (Notre-Dame de la Treille) was soon drawing pilgrims. The medieval city grew up as a densely populated network of narrow streets and canals around the Motte, the fortified feudal castle mound (roughly where Notre-Dame de la Treille is today), the Comtal Palace of the counts of Flanders and the Collégiale St-Pierre, on the site of the present Palais de Justice.

Lille's position on trade routes made it one of the great wool towns of Flanders, along with Douai, Ypres, Ghent and Bruges, and part of the Hanseatic League. Soon Lille became the centre of an important annual medieval fair that drew merchants from all over Europe, trading in agricultural products, wool and textiles, and exporting fine woollen cloth to southern France, Italy, Spain and Portugal. The town outgrew its earliest fortifications, absorbing the church of St-Maurice and, later in the 13th century, the three parishes of St-Sauveur, Ste-Catherine and St-André, with the construction of a new set of walls.

In the early Middle Ages, Flanders was nominally under the rule of the French crown, but in practice the powerful Count of Flanders ruled a quasi-independent state. Lille's growing prosperity made it an attractive prize in the constant struggle for dominance in a Franco-Flemish rivalry that was to set the pattern for centuries. The Flemish counts had a palace somewhere near the Palais de Justice; the French monarchy built an imposing fortress near to where the Porte de Gand stands today. In 1213 Philippe Auguste besieged the city of Lille, and in 1214 his victory at the Battle of Bouvines, just to the south, against the alliance of King John of England, the Count of Flanders and the Holy Roman Emperor, briefly asserted French power.

The kitchen of the Musée de l'Hospice Comtesse

The town had its own militia, the Confrérie Ste-Barbe or Canonniers Sédentaires to defend it, and minted its own money (on rue de la Monnaie). Under the patronage of nobles and wealthy merchants, hospices – charity hospitals for the elderly and indigent – also flourished, including the Hôpital Notre-Dame (today the Musée de l'Hospice Comtesse), founded by the Comtesse Jeanne in 1237.

A Sip of Burgundy

In 1369, with the marriage of Marguerite de Flandres, the daughter of the Count of Flanders, to Philippe le Hardi, Duke of Burgundy, Flanders came under Burgundian rule. Lille became one of the jewels of the powerful duchy, on a par with Dijon and Brussels. Sometimes it was allied with England, sometimes with France, during the Hundred Years War, a time in which the town was hit by both war and plague. Philippe le Hardi and his successor Jean Sans Peur built solid new ramparts dotted with impregnable towers of which only the Noble Tour remains today.

In 1453 Philippe le Bon began building a grandiose ducal palace, the Palais Rihour, symbol of a new period of prosperity for the town. Lille was the favourite part of his domain, a flourishing centre of the arts and also of chivalry – it was here he summoned the knights of the Ordre de la Toison d'Or

(Order of the Golden Fleece) for the sumptuous Banquet du Faisan in 1454. The feast lasted several days and a succession of grandiose courses – exotic fruits, roast swans and peacocks, elaborate desserts – was interspersed with entertainers, musicians and dramatic scenes recounting the story of Jason and the Golden Fleece. At the end of the meal, the duke and his vassals all swore allegiance to a golden pheasant, splendidly attired in a gold collar studded with precious stones.

Northern Artists

In the 15th and 16th centuries Lille was very much a part of the northern Renaissance and the golden age of Flemish painting, with its early use of oil paint, skill at portraiture and the combination of meticulous detail and luminous northern skies. Artists such as Rogier Van der Weyden, born in nearby Tournai, Hans Memling and Jan Van Eyck worked for the Dukes of Burgundy in Beaune and probably also for the ducal court at the Palais Rihour in Lille. The town corporations and religious foundations and monasteries were also wealthy patrons.

Douai-born Jean de Bellegambe (c1470–1534) painted several sensitive altarpieces, which can be seen today in museums in Lille, Douai and Arras. Although mannerist sculptor Giambologna is more usually associated with Florence, he too was born in Douai and trained in Flanders. Later, in the 17th century, Rubens was commissioned by the Couvent des Capucines to paint an altarpiece for its chapel (today in the Palais des Beaux-Arts), just one of several altarpieces commissioned from Rubens and his pupils Van Dyck and Jordaens by the Catholic Church, which used prestigious painters to promote the Counter-Reformation against the Protestantism of the Netherlands to the north. Even Valenciennes-born Jean-Antoine Watteau, master of French rococo style in the early 18th century, lies in the Flemish tradition, with his delicate, thin use of paint; his nephew Louis Watteau and Louis's son François, were based in Lille and specialised in painting Lille festivities.

Spanish Rule

The 17th-century Vieille Bourse

In 1492 Flanders fell under the rule of the house of Habsburg. With the marriage of the son of Marie de Bourgogne and Maximilien of Austria, to the Infanta of Spain, it passed to the control of the Spanish monarchy, in an empire that included Spain, the Low Countries, Austria and Germany. Exterior power was lessened, and the fiercely independent magistrature – the equivalent of the city council – demolished both the old Flemish palace and the French castle in the early 16th century, though it still needed permission from the Emperor for the city, which was bursting at the seams, to expand. In the early 17th century, land was annexed north and west of the ducal palace, and new fortifications went up, in the shape of the Porte de Gand and Porte de Roubaix.

In the 1650s Philip IV of Spain granted permission for the construction of a new trading exchange, the Bourse des Marchands (now the Vieille Bourse), a new demonstration of mercantile strength. A number of buildings from this period have been preserved, but one aspect has gone forever: the old city used to be criss-crossed by canals, which have been filled in or covered over and left to dry up in the cellars of later buildings.

The French Conquest

In the 17th century, powerful Louis XIV decided to take matters in hand to regain this corner for France, claiming legitimacy to Spanish Flanders after his marriage in 1660 to Maria Teresa of Spain. In 1667, after a nine-day siege, the city finally capitulated, and Louis XIV sent in his brilliant military architect Sébastien Le Prestre de Vauban to transform the city and make it the centre of his military strategy for the north. On the marshy land northwest of the existing city, the star-shaped Citadelle was built at the centre of a vast system of walls and defensive ditches and canals. Vauban's star-shaped fortresses dotted what are now northern France, Flanders and the southern Netherlands. A new district, the Quartier Royale, also went up with streets laid out on a grid plan, while in 1673 the grandiose new Porte de Paris, glorifying the king's martial victories, replaced the old gate. In 1713 under the Treaty of Utrecht, Lille remained French, but Tournai, Courtrai and Ypres were returned to the Netherlands.

Lille Besieged

The French Revolution of 1789 was a fairly low-key affair in Lille. Monasteries toppled, churches became temples of reason, the new calendar beginning with the year I was brought in, but the town escaped the blood-letting of Paris. However, the actions of the revolutionary *assemblée* in the capital were to have major consequences for Lille. In 1792 the legislative assembly declared war on the royalist Austrian-held Low Countries, and Lille, as a frontier town, was in the firing line. Mayor André led the town's resistance to a siege by the Austrian army.

Boom Time

New machinery and the introduction of steam power in the 1820s and, above all, the invention of the steam loom transformed the textile industry, aided by the development of the nearby coal mines. Rural migrants from France and Belgium flocked to the textile cities, and Lille – and Roubaix and Tourcoing even more so – expanded at an unprecedented rate.

Column, commemorating the 1792 siege, in Lille's Grand' Place

While Roubaix and Tourcoing made wool, Lille was important for linen (flax was a major crop in the area and is still grown today), lacemaking and cotton. Other industries included tanning, brassmaking, tobacco processing and sugar refining (Napoleon had encouraged the cultivation of sugar beet in the north when France was blockaded from supplies of sugar cane). In 1846 the railway arrived from Paris and gradually supplanted transport by canal. In 1867 the factory of the iron company Lille-Fives was opened by Napoleon III, soon employing 3,000 workers who were building locomotives and iron bridges for use across the French empire.

But the city desperately needed more room to house its workers, who often lived crowded into insalubrious cellars. An estimated 80 percent of the population worked in the textile industry, including many children. After epidemics of cholera in 1832 and 1849, the city was at last given permission to expand once again. In 1858 the old city walls were demolished, and the nearby villages of Wazemmes, Moulins, Esquermes, Fives and St-Maurice were absorbed into the city, doubling the population. A new set of ramparts was built further out, punctuated by forts, such as those that still stand at Mons-en-Barœul and Bondues.

Under the Second Empire of Napoleon III the new Préfecture was built, and Parisian-style boulevards were laid out, lined with fanciful houses for the city's industrial barons. New parks were landscaped with romantic lakes and grottoes, while factories often took on the air of castles. This is also the period when the city's two universities (the Université de Lille and the Université Catholique) were built; illustrious professors included Louis Pasteur. In the new century the Théâtre de Solférino, the Opéra de Lille and Lille's first department store all came into being.

Palais des Beaux-Arts on place de la République, the epitome of grandiose 19th-century town planning

War and Politics

When World War I broke out in 1914, Lille had long outgrown its fortifications. It was declared a 'ville ouverte' – meaning that it was not going to be defended, although French troops did put up a resistance. The Siege of Lille began on 2 September 1914, and on 13 October the town submitted after heavy bombardment by artillery. The German occupation was a period of hardship, as the population starved. Hundreds of buildings were destroyed in the town centre – the Palais Rihour was gutted in 1916 except for the chapel, which is now used as the Office de Tourisme – though much of Vieux Lille escaped.

Lille's politicians have played a role on the national stage. Roger Salengro, mayor of Lille from 1925, was interior minister during Léon Blum's 1936-elected Front Populaire – France's first and short-lived socialist government. Pierre Mauroy, mayor of Lille from 1973 to 2001 and current president of Lille Métropole, was French prime minister under François Mitterrand from 1981 to 1984, while his successor as mayor of Lille, Martine Aubrey, is a former interior minister.

With its industrial history, the north was a stronghold of French socialism and the testing ground for many new social advances: France's first socialist co-operative was set up in Roubaix in 1885, followed by a similar workers' association in Lille; the *Internationale* revolutionary hymn was composed by Pierre Degeyter in Lille in 1888.

With World War II, the north was once again occupied and put under the German command in Brussels. In April 1944, 86 villagers in Ascq were executed in reprisals by SS troops arriving from the Russian front. The city was liberated on 2 September of that same year.

Sculpture by Yayoi Kusama

International Crossroads

The 1950s and 1960s saw the closure of the region's mines and a decline in the textile industry, nevertheless, 1970 saw the foundation of the town of Villeneuve d'Ascq. In 1983 the VAL, the world's first driverless Métro system, was inaugurated, and, in 1987, Lille Métropole was created, comprising the four cities of Lille, Roubaix, Tourcoing and Villeneuve d'Ascq, a host of smaller towns and villages, as well as industrial areas and rural farmland. The vision of Pierre Mauroy, then-mayor of Lille, went even further. He looked forward to cross-frontier exchanges with Belgium, as well as Great Britain, linked since 1994 by the Channel Tunnel, promoting Lille as an international crossroads between France, Britain, Belgium, the Netherlands and Germany.

The north remains one of the poorest parts of France, yet Lille has become an island of prosperity and dynamism, even if it hasn't quite regained the prestige of its heyday. Lille Métropole remains France's leading textile manufacturer, with Roubaix now producing innovative technological fabrics, as well as being an important centre for printing, food industries and the service sector. Lille's selection as European Capital of Culture in 2004 spurred the renaissance on. From this came the renovation of several monuments, landscaping projects, a prestigious arts programme and a new international visibility. Building work continues apace with the extension of Euralille, and the city strives to maintain its cultural momentum through Lille 3000, a new biennial cultural festival; the first of which, running from October 2006 to January 2007, is devoted to India.

Historical Landmarks

1066 First mention of L'Isle (the island) in a charter.
1347–52 Black Death wipes out two-thirds of the population of Europe.
1369 Marriage of Marguerite, Countess of Flanders, to Philippe le Hardi, Duke of Burgundy, brings the city under Burgundian control.
1402–22 New ramparts, including Noble Tour, built.
1469 Charter grants town of Roubaix the right to produce woollen cloth.
1477 Marriage of Marie de Bourgogne to Maximilien of Austria.
Late 15th century Flanders passes to Spanish rule.
1620–21 Porte de Roubaix and Porte de Gand built as part of the city wall.
1651–3 Vieille Bourse built.
1667 Louis XIV takes Lille.
1670 Vauban builds the Citadelle.
1708–13 Lille occupied by the Dutch in the War of the Spanish Succession.
1789 French Revolution.
1790 Département of the Nord created from former Flanders.
1792 Lille besieged by the Austrian army.
1804 Beginning of mechanisation of textile industry.
1854 Louis Pasteur founds the Science Faculty at the Université de Lille.
1858 City ramparts are demolished, and the villages of Wazemmes, Fives, Moulins, Esquermes and St-Maurice are incorporated within the city.
1896 First Paris–Roubaix cycling race.
1914–18 World War I. Large parts of central Lille destroyed. Lille occupied.
1944 April massacre of 86 villagers at Ascq; Lille liberated on 2 September.
1970 Creation of new town of Villeneuve d'Ascq.
1983 VAL, the world's first fully automated, driverless Métro system, opens.
1987 Creation of Lille Métropole, linking Lille, Villeneuve d'Ascq, Tourcoing, Roubaix and 83 other communes into a large urban district.
1994 Opening of the Channel Tunnel, sending Eurostar traffic through Lille.
1996 Beginning of work on the Euralille district.
1999 Completion of the Cathédrale Notre-Dame de la Treille.
2004 Lille is Cultural Capital of Europe.
2006 Launch of the Lille 3000 biennale.

A la Cloche d'Or
LEON BOUTRY
BIJOUTERIE

WHERE TO GO

Lille has come a long way since its humble beginnings as a small island on the River Deûle, notably as a major industrial centre in the 19th century and a dynamic cultural showcase at the start of the 21st. This arresting development, coupled with the city's status as a fought-over border town, pervades its architecture, art collections, cuisine and culture, offering much to the visitor. The best place to start a tour is the heart of the old city, Vieux Lille. From there, head out to the adjacent central areas and, if time allows, the surrounding suburbs. For those wishing to explore the area around Lille, we suggest short hops over the border and the best excursions further afield.

VIEUX LILLE

Vieux Lille is Lille at its most delightful: well-preserved streets of narrow brick-and-stone Flemish houses, many recently restored and now containing upmarket shops, regional restaurants and lively bars that point to the city's recent renaissance as well as its historic one. Two of Vieux Lille's main sights – the Vieille Bourse and Musée de l'Hospice Comtesse – date from Lille's glorious past; a third, the Cathédrale Notre-Dame de la Treille, is a more recent curiosity.

On top of the column in the Grand' Place, the figure of La Déesse commemorates the city's heroic stand and deliverance from the Austrian siege in 1792. Legend has it that the rather grumpy-looking goddess was modelled on the wife of the mayor.

Grand' Place

➤ The heart of the city is the original medieval market square, the **Grand' Place** (officially called place Général de Gaulle), which is still a

A la Cloche d'Or, Vieux Lille

popular meeting place and centre of festivities. In the middle, on top of a fluted column, stands a statue of **La Déesse** (the Goddess), who was credited with saving the city during a siege by Austrian troops in 1792. The square is now semi-pedestrianised, with tables from the brasseries Le Coq Hardi and La Houblonnière spreading over the pavement. On one side is La Vieille Bourse *(see opposite)*, generally considered to be Lille's finest building. At the end of the square, with an elegant double staircase, the Grand-Garde was built to hold the royal guard and is now home to the **Théâtre du Nord**. Note the sunburst motif of the pediment in tribute to Louis XIV, though the building dates from 1717, two years after the Sun King's death. Next to it is the striking 1930s' building of the **Voix du Nord** regional newspaper, with its Flemish-style stepped gable, modernist reliefs and three golden muses on the pinnacle; downstairs now contains a FNAC book-and-music

The Vieille Bourse, considered to be Lille's finest building

The Opéra, with the belfry of the Nouvelle Bourse adjacent

shop. Take a look also at **A la Cloche d'Or**, a pretty *belle-époque* shopfront with fanciful ironwork. Opposite the Vieille Bourse, the Furet du Nord, one of the largest bookshops in Europe, is a local landmark, though its name – *furet* means ferret – stems from a furrier previously on the premises.

If one building sums up the city's Flemish glory it is the **Vieille Bourse**, with its polychrome façade of red brick, grey stone and carved golden stone. The exterior is sumptuously decorated with sculpted caryatids and windows with broken pediments, and the courtyard with richly carved swags of fruit and extraordinarily expressive grimacing masks and scowling monsters above the arcades. The Vieille Bourse was built in 1651–3 by architect Julien Destrée, after permission was granted to the town by Philip IV of Spain to build a Stock Exchange for mercantile trading. Despite its uniform appearance, it is actually composed of 24 houses with shops on the ground floor, built round an arcaded interior courtyard that is now used by second-hand booksellers, with an entrance from the street on each side. Inside the ground-floor arcades, the windows were replaced in the 19th century by a celebration of France's scientists and industrialists, such as the geologist Brongniart, physicist and chemist Gay Lussac, Jacquard (inventor of the Jacquard loom) and Pasteur, who began his experiments on fermentation in Lille when doyen of the science faculty.

On the other side of the Vieille Bourse, on place du Théâtre, the **Opéra de Lille**, designed by Louis-Marie Cordonnier, was inaugurated in 1923 to replace the old 18th-century opera house, which had burnt down in 1903. The classical façade crowned by an exuberant statue of Apollo and the Muses, the grandiose foyer and lavishly gilded auditorium were all beautifully restored in 2002–3. As well as being used for opera, concerts and ballet, the building is open during the day for visits, for a drink or snack in the café and for art installations.

Next to the Opéra is the **Nouvelle Bourse**, designed by the same architect as the Opéra, at roughly the same date but in a quite different style, marking a neo-vernacular revival that harks back to the city's Flemish past in its ornate use of red brick and white stone, its gabled roof and its tall belfry, a symbol of civic pride. Opposite, the **Rang de Beauregard** is a fine terrace of 14 tall and narrow, late-17th-century houses, designed by Simon Vollant; it set a model for the new regulations controlling architectural style and the uniformity of façades

Taking time out at a café near the Grand' Place

introduced under Louis XIV. However, there was still plenty of room for the local love of sculpted decoration, seen here in angels, cherubs, masks and cornucopias.

Mosaics, A l'Huîtrière

North of the Grand' Place

Upmarket fashion boutiques, shoe stores and jewellers abound on rue de la Grande Chaussée and rue des Chats Bossus – two of the city's earliest thoroughfares, which originally led from the market place to the port. You can't miss **A l'Huîtrière** *(see page 135)*, at 3 rue des Chats Bossus, Lille's grandest restaurant-cum-fishmonger, thanks to its fabulous 1928 art deco mosaic façade by Breton artist Mathurin Meheut. Peek through the windows to see fresh fish, shellfish and other gourmet goodies, and tiled scenes of fishermen.

There are several fine Flemish Renaissance and baroque houses in typical red brick and carved stone in this part of Lille, notably on place du Lion d'Or and **place Louise de Bettignies**. Several have been repainted in warm ochres and russsets, which were probably the sort of colours used in the past.

The most ostentatious of all these houses is on the corner of place Louise de Bettignies and avenue de la Peuple Belge. Erected in 1636 for wealthy grocer Gilles de la Boë, it has an arcaded ground floor, where goods were once unloaded from boats, and an abundantly decorated first floor, laden with jutting cornices, cartouches, scrolls, grapes and other motifs. De la Boë's house originally overlooked the Port de Rivage, the ancient port, for as recently as the 1930s the grassy centre of the broad avenue de la Peuple Belge was the Canal de la

Pâtisserie Méert

Basse-Deûle and the current roads were once quaysides where boats unloaded their wares. Today, the only hint of the avenue's watery past is the Pont Neuf bridge that crosses over it further down.

There are plenty of other fine façades to ogle at while window shopping in Vieux Lille. On rue Basse, stop to admire No. 34, dated 1761, with its rococo wrought-iron balconies and sculpted window surrounds, and No. 41, dated 1651; rue Basse heads back towards rue Esquermoise, home to **Méert** *(see box, page 102)*, a pâtisserie and salon de thé that has become a Lille landmark. Other sights include rue de Weppes, once a canal, and cobbled rue des Vieux-Murs, rue Pélerinck and the pretty place aux Oignons, which form a knot of terraced weavers' cottages, now restored and containing quirky shops. Oignons is thought to be a corruption of *donjon*, referring to the nearby keep, rather than anything to do with onions.

Porte de Gand

From place Louise de Bettignies, restaurant-packed rue de Gand – a popular night-time destination – leads to the **Porte de Gand**, one of two fortified gateways (with the Porte de Roubaix) to survive the expansion of the city in the 1620s. Although the gateways still had a defensive purpose (note the slits either side of the coat-of-arms from where the portcullis used to be raised), they were also a way of displaying the city's prestige (the arches were originally single but two more openings were added for the tramway in the 19th century), with coats-of-arms and statuary. On the town side, the Porte de Gand has herringbone-pattern brickwork; it is now home to a fashionable restaurant, Les Terraces des Remparts. Outside the gate, mounds, ramparts and ditches date from Vauban's rebuilding of Lille's military defences half a century later.

A couple of streets south of the Porte de Gand, the curious **Musée des Canonniers Sédentaires de Lille** (entrance rue des Urbanistes; open Mon–Sat 2–7pm, closed mid-Dec to mid-Feb and first three weeks of Aug) occupies an 18th-century convent. Arms, cannons, paintings, engravings and other memorabilia tell the story of the Ste-Barbe cannon battalion, a sort of local militia, that has defended Lille since 1235. The dates of the numerous times the city was besieged are listed over the doorway on rue des Canonniers.

Porte de Roubaix

Southeast from here, the recently restored **Porte de Roubaix** leads through to the Parc Henri Matisse and views of the Euralille district *(see page 52)*. Between the Porte de Roubaix and the Gare Lille Flandres is a more rundown, as yet ungentrified, area of Vieux Lille. On rue de Roubaix, take a look at the grandiose entrance façade of the Hôtel D'Hailly d'Aigremont (if you're lucky the gates may open to reveal the fine 18th-century *hôtel particulier*, or private mansion, at the rear of the courtyard, and now a general's residence). Nearby, the plaque on rue du Lombard, in tribute to former resident 'A D Scrive-Labbe, Lille industrialist 1789–1864, who at the risk of his life imported from England to Lille the first carding machine...' suggests that industrial progress was not always welcome.

Musée de l'Hospice Comtesse

Rue de la Monnaie, which runs north along the course of an ancient medieval lane from place Louise de Bettignies to the palace of the Count of Flanders, is full of upmarket shops. Here, too, is the lovely **Musée de l'Hospice Comtesse** (32 rue de la Monnaie; open Mon 2–6pm, Wed–Sun 10am–12.30pm, 2–6pm). The Hospice was founded in 1237 by the Countess Jeanne of Flanders, who ruled the city while her husband, Fernand of Portugal, was imprisoned in the Louvre. A religious foundation, the Hospice Comtesse was a powerful, wealthy institution for centuries (it remained in use as an orphanage and old people's hospital until 1939), as it controlled rights to all the flour mills in the city. Today, it is an atmospheric, intimate museum, which gives a picture both of the charity hospitals that were such an important feature in Flanders, and of local decorative arts and history.

The buildings, most of which date from the 17th and 18th centuries, are arranged around a cobbled courtyard reached from the street through a fine vaulted archway. Nuns' quarters are on one side, the chapel and sick ward on another. You go in through the kitchen, which has walls totally covered in blue-and-white Delft-style tiles made in Lille in the 18th century, painted with scenes of people fishing, children playing, whales, windmills and other motifs. Other rooms, such as the refectory (containing a long table, richly carved dressers and religious paintings), the panelled parlour and the linen room (with genre paintings and blue-and-white glazed earthenware) give a picture both of life in the Hospice and of local decorative arts. There are several paintings by Arnould de Vuez (c1644–1719), who also painted the altarpiece and the cycle of the *Life of the Virgin* in the chapel. Upstairs, the former nuns' dormitory contains items reflecting Lille's history, including wood carvings and portraits, and, notably, two paintings of the Braderie de Lille and a procession of trade guilds in 1789 by Louis Watteau (nephew of Jean-Antoine Watteau) and his son François, both of whom specialised in depicting local festivities.

Around the Cathedral

The other principal sight in Vieux Lille can be reached through a small passageway from rue de la Monnaie, or by a number of small streets that lead off rue Basse. Curious rather than beautiful, Lille's cathedral **Notre-Dame de la Treille** (open Mon–Sat 10am–noon, 2–6pm, Sun 10am–1pm, 3–6pm, 7pm in summer) is named after a miracle-performing statue of the Virgin that used to draw pilgrims to Lille in the Middle Ages. Building was begun in the 19th century on the site of the original medieval motte-and-bailey castle: the grassy square outside is still surrounded by a deep ditch on the trace of the old moat, with little bridges crossing into the gardens of surrounding houses. Money ran out halfway through construction of the cathedral, and for decades the building stood unfinished, its surrounding square a sort of wasteland. Work began again in the 1990s, and the cathedral was finally inaugurated in 1999, 145 years after it was begun. Rather than continuing the neo-Gothic style of the previous century, a

Rose window by Kijno, Notre-Dame de la Treille

At 61 rue de la Monnaie, wander into the courtyard to take a look at the elegant 18th-century Hôtel de la Monnaie, where coins were minted in the Middle Ages and the king's money was stored until the 19th century. The building now houses the restaurant L'Assiette du Marché *(see page 136)*.

resolutely modern solution of minimalist grey marble within a steel grid was chosen. From the exterior, the stark grey façade seems cold and forbidding, especially in daytime, but inside the result is genuinely surprising and much more welcoming. From within, the new west front appears to be translucent, the marble glowing a streaky, pinky-orange, with a modern rose window by Kijno set in a frame of light. To the right of the transept, a fine 15th-century altarpiece depicts the *Mystère de la Roseraie* (Mystery of the Rosary).

A little further up rue de la Monnaie, a food market is held on **place du Concert** on Wednesday, Friday and Sunday mornings; stalls are set up around the statue of Mayor André, who refused to surrender the town during the Austrian siege in 1792. On opposite sides of rue Colas, which runs along the side of the square, are the modern Conservatoire de Musique and the Palais de Justice.

South of the cathedral, rue St-Etienne and rue de Pas are home to a number of good restaurants. Take a look at the glazed-in front courtyard of **La Compostelle** (4 rue St-Etienne, *see page 137*), in the 1572 Hôtel de Beaurepaire, once a pilgrims' halt on the route to Compostella, hence the cockle-shell motif carved above the door. The arcaded stone façade is a rare example of the more classical, sober French Renaissance style with shallow-relief motifs, as opposed to the opulently carved version adored in Flanders. Nearby, the circular 1960s' **Nouveau Siècle** is home to the highly reputed Orchestre National de Lille.

Quartier Royale

Unlike the narrow, winding streets and irregular squares of the heart of Vieux Lille, the **Quartier Royale** was a new district laid out under Louis XIV on a geometric grid to connect the old city to the new Citadelle. Begun in 1670 by Vauban, its hierarchy of streets reflects the French love of order: grand brick terraces were built on rue Royale and parallel rue St-André, while simpler houses were built on perpendicular streets, such as rue d'Angleterre, rue de Jemmapes and rue Princesse.

Today, the southern end of rue Royale has some of the city's trendiest bars, but towards the Citadelle, it is still lined with fine 18th-century *hôtels particuliers*, erected by the nobility who had followed the monarch to Lille. These private mansions often followed the Parisian fashion of having an elegant gateway opening on to the street, with the main residence hidden at the back of a gracious entrance courtyard and a sweeping garden behind. Many are now offices, but during the week you can often get glimpses of the grand residences behind, such as the Hôtel de Lamissart (No. 130) with a neo-classical entrance of pilasters and urns, the Hôtel Van der Cruisse de Waziers at No. 95, the Hôtel de Hespil (now the Banque de France) at No. 75 and, facing it, the bishop's palace. On the corner of rues

Hôtel de Lamissart, rue Royale

Royale and Princesse, opposite the Hôtel de Lamissart is the early 18th-century Jesuit church of **St-André** (open Wed, Fri and 1st and 3rd Sat of each month 1–5pm), whose brick tower was added in the 1890s. Just beyond the church, the

Queen of Citadelles

Symbol of Louis XIV's capture of the town in 1667 and lynchpin of his military strategy for control of northern France, the new Citadelle designed by the king's military engineer Sébastien Le Prestre de Vauban and his assistant, architect Simon Vollant, is the largest in France. What Vauban himself called the 'Queen of Citadelles' took only three years to build, using 2,000 labourers. Situated on marshy land northeast of the city, the Citadelle follows a star-shaped plan, with five bastions, a series of concentric ramparts and water-filled ditches. It was a veritable town within the town, home to a large garrison and with all the services – from bakery to brewery – necessary for withstanding a long siege. An imposing stone gateway, the Porte Royale, leads into the heart of the Citadelle, where the barracks, chapel and arsenal are arranged around a large pentagonal central courtyard. Today, the Citadelle is a curious mix of leafy public park and strictly off-limits military property, which can be visited only on guided tours (May–Aug Sun 3pm, meet at the Porte Royale, bring passport or ID card) organised by the Office de Tourisme, or for the *Journées du Patrimoine (see page 97)* in September.

Outside the ramparts, within a loop of the Deûle, the Bois de Boulogne is a grassy, wooded area with footpaths and a fitness circuit. On one side, the Champ de Mars, once a military parade ground, is now a car park. Nearby, there is a small children's playground and the free Zoo (open summer 9am–5.30pm, Sat, Sun till 6.30pm; winter 10am–4pm, Sat, Sun till 5pm, closed 2nd Sun in Dec–2nd Sun in Feb; <www.zoolille.com>), which is popular with Lillois at weekends. An easy circuit takes in monkeys on a little island, lemurs and marmosets, zebras and rhinos, as well as exotic birds and a reptile house.

Zebras at Lille Zoo

forbidding Grand Magasin was built as a grain warehouse in the 1720s and was long the highest building in the city. At the time of writing it was empty and awaiting redevelopment.

Back towards the Grand' Place on rue Ste-Catherine, **Eglise Ste-Catherine** (open Tues, Thur and 2nd and 4th Sat of each month 1–5pm) is one of the city's oldest churches, with fine Gothic windows, three equal naves and a solid, truncated tower that served as a watchtower. Concerts are sometimes staged here. In the surrounding square, look at the curious house at No. 5, which has Egyptian motifs on its façade from when ancient Egypt came into fashion following Napoleon's Egyptian Campaign. Behind here, there are several fine houses on rue de la Barre, with a mix of 18th-century *hôtels particuliers* and much earlier buildings.

At the end of the street, the Bassin St-Martin and the tranquil, cobbled quai de Wault are rare reminders of the extensive network of canals that used to cross Lille. On the quayside, the former **Couvent des Minimes** is now an upmarket hotel with rooms built around a beautiful 17th-century rib-vaulted cloister. The canal formerly continued under what are now squares Dutilleul and Foch, both laid out in the 19th century. At the junction of square Foch and rue Nationale, the white marble statue of the *P'tit Quinquin*, illustrating a popular lullaby about a poor lacemaker and her baby, is a masterpiece of 19th-century pathos.

Situated on the northeastern border of the Quartier Royale, on rue du Pont Neuf, the deconsecrated church of

Bust of Charles de Gaulle at his birthplace museum

Ste-Marie-Madeleine is a rare example in northern France of the domed baroque style. Constructed during the late 17th century to give the then-new district of Lille a symbol of church power, it is designed on a square Greek cross plan with aisles radiating off a circular choir under the outsize, 37-m (121-ft) high dome and lantern. Recently restored, the church has been used for art installations since 2004.

Maison Natale Charles de Gaulle

Northwest of here, at 9 rue Princesse, is the **Maison Natale Charles de Gaulle** (open Wed–Sun 10am–noon, 2–5pm), where the French wartime resistance leader and later president, Charles de Gaulle, was born in his grandmother's house on 22 November 1890. Items on display include his cradle, christening robe, letters, photographs and a uniform made in London's Savile Row during World War II – showing that de Gaulle was particularly tall. The panelled rooms and mahogany furniture give a picture of the lifestyle of a comfortably-off bourgeois family at the end of the 19th century. The home spreads across three terraced houses and originally had industrial premises at the rear, where de Gaulle's grandfather had introduced a new method of making fine tulle gauze. Across the courtyard is an audiovisual space, with interactive multimedia terminals, and archive photographic exhibits relating to World War II and de Gaulle.

ST-SAUVEUR

Gare Lille Flandres and Eglise St-Maurice

Composer Hector Berlioz came in person to conduct his *Chant des Chemins de Fer* (Railway Chorus) to celebrate the opening of the railway between Paris and Lille in 1846. He arrived by train at the new **Gare Lille Flandres**, its façade partly rebuilt from the old Paris Gare du Nord (the vault over the tracks was added in the 1880s). The station elegantly crowns rue Faidherbe, the shopping street that leads to the Grand' Place.

Behind the station, on avenue Willy Brandt, the huge red-brick **Tri Postal** (postal sorting office) was converted into an exhibition centre and party venue for Lille 2004, and is now used for art exhibitions and rock concerts.

Gare Lille Flandres

The area around the station is a typical hinterland of budget hotels, kebab shops and pavement brasseries, but it is also home to Lille's finest church, **Eglise St-Maurice** (open Mon 1.15–6pm, Tues–Sat 10.15am–12.15pm, 1.15–6pm, Sun 3.30–6pm). This large, late Gothic structure in pale creamy stone has grown over several centuries – it was begun in the 14th on the site of a much earlier church, and completed in the 19th with an ornate west front and spire – but is typical of the tall *hallekerkes* of Flanders

Eglise St-Maurice, built from the 14th to 19th centuries

and the Netherlands. Its five equal naves and slender columns were designed to spread the weight evenly over marshy terrain, and give an impression of space and light that is reinforced by the clear glass along the nave windows. The end chapel is dedicated to the defence of Lille by the Canonniers Bourgeois.

Hôtel de Ville and St-Sauveur District

Stretching south of the Gare Lille Flandres, the St-Sauveur district, centred on the original medieval thoroughfares rue de Paris and rue St-Sauveur, was long notorious for its insalubrious slums. Today it is a mixture of historic remnants, 1920s' and 1930s' reconstruction and recent developments.

➤ The **Hôtel de Ville**, built 1924–32, replaced the previous town hall, located in the medieval Palais Rihour (now the tourist office) when this was partially destroyed in World War I. Emile Dubuisson's design expressed both modernity and regional identity, marking a revival in neo-Flemish vernacular in its gabled roof and use of red brick and reinforced concrete, and also the streamlined linearity of art deco. Standing next to it is a soaring 104m (340ft) belfry, with stylised sculptures of Lille's mythical giants Lydéric and Phineart around the base *(see page 13)*.

Facing the Hôtel de Ville, at the end of rue de Paris (and today located in the centre of a busy roundabout), the **Porte de Paris**, or Paris Gateway, is the most flamboyant of all Louis XIV's embellishments to Lille. It was built by Simon Vollant from 1685 to 1692 as a fortified gateway and triumphal arch to celebrate Louis XIV's capture of the town.

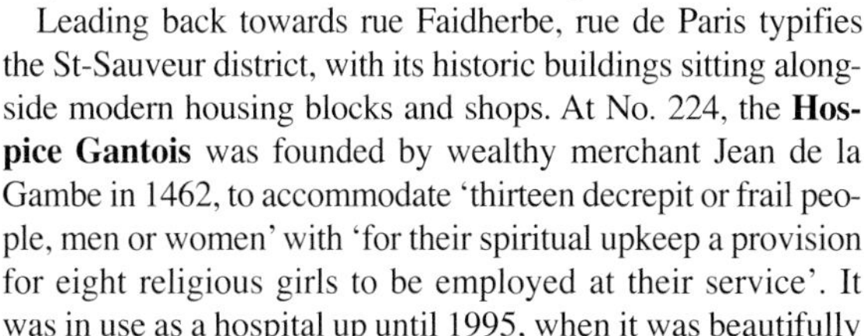

Leading back towards rue Faidherbe, rue de Paris typifies the St-Sauveur district, with its historic buildings sitting alongside modern housing blocks and shops. At No. 224, the **Hospice Gantois** was founded by wealthy merchant Jean de la Gambe in 1462, to accommodate 'thirteen decrepit or frail people, men or women' with 'for their spiritual upkeep a provision for eight religious girls to be employed at their service'. It was in use as a hospital up until 1995, when it was beautifully

Belfries

Belfries are one of the most visible features of northern towns. Eleven of them have recently been given World Heritage Status by UNESCO. Prominent landmarks in a flat landscape, they were once both a source of civic pride – symbolising the power of burghers and corporations, as opposed to the church or nobility – and a watchtower, from which the bell would be rung in case of attack. Belfries continued to be built long after their defensive role died out: Lille's two belfries, at the Hôtel de Ville and the Nouvelle Bourse, date from the 20th century. In Comines, Armentières and Wattrelos, according to tradition, the mayor climbs the belfry once a year to throw biscuits to his citizens. The particularly fine belfries at Béthune, Armentières, Bergues, Dunkerque and Douai can be climbed.

restored as the Hermitage Gantois, a restaurant and luxury hotel that opened in 2003. From the street, you can still see the gable of the original 16th-century sickroom. Even if you are not staying there, it is worth going inside to look at the panelled chapel, tiled, barrel-vaulted ward and series of trim courtyard gardens. Further along the street, renovation continues: a block of 17th-century houses with sculpted dolphin motifs has been incorporated into the modern Les Tanneurs shopping centre.

Behind the Hôtel de Ville, an arcaded pavilion remains from the 18th-century **Hôpital St-Sauveur**, with stone pilasters and swags and an ornate carved doorway. Next to it stands the heavy, 19th-century, neo-Byzantine **Eglise St-Sauveur**, with a curious domed tower.

Surrounded by flats and a school, the massive, 2-m (6½-ft) wide walls of the squat **Noble Tour** are all that remain of the medieval city wall. Once the highest of 65 towers that encircled the city, the tower was built in the early 15th century – to keep out the French – by Philip the Bold, Duke of Burgundy, allied to the English in the Hundred Years War. On the exterior, a modern bronze sculpture of a man in chains by Bizette-Lindon is a memorial to the World War II Résistance.

PALAIS RIHOUR AND RÉPUBLIQUE

Palais Rihour

➤ Sticking out among the brasseries of place Rihour, the **Palais Rihour** (open Mon–Sat 9.30am–6.30pm, Sun 10am–noon, 2–5pm), now home to the tourist office, is all that remains of the once sumptuous palace of the dukes of Burgundy begun by Philippe le Bon (Philip the Bold) in 1453. It became the city hall in the 17th century, and was damaged by fire during the 18th century, only to be almost completely destroyed in World War I – the original palace would have occupied what is now the entire square. The tourist office itself is in the vaulted former Salle des Gardes, while, reached up a vaulted staircase with foliate capitals, the Salle de Conclave (the original chapel and later municipal congress room) is often open for exhibitions. You can admire its ribbed vaulting, and a Gothic doorway leads into a small sacristy with stained glass. A 1920s' war memorial is built into one side of the building.

The austere-looking **Eglise St-Etienne** (open Mon–Sat 2–5pm, Sun 10am–noon, 2.30–5pm) on rue de l'Hôpital Militaire was built in the 18th century on the model of the Jesuit churches of the Counter-Reformation. The interior is more ornate, notably the richly sculpted 1820s' wooden pulpit by François Rude, best known as the sculptor of *La Marseillaise* on the Arc de Triomphe in Paris. At the base stand large figures of Hope and Religion, on the pulpit a frieze depicts the stoning of St Stephen, while the canopy is surmounted by an archangel and cherubs. In the chancel there are *trompe-l'oeil* murals of

Art deco buildings on rue de Béthune, south of place Rihour

architectural perspectives and two unusual 18th-century reliquaries in silver-plated copper in the form of saints' busts. Next door, the adjoining convent buildings, long a military hospital, are currently being converted into offices for the Préfecture.

Nearby, the pedestrianised area around **rue de Béthune**, with shops, cinemas and the 1930s' brasserie Aux Moules *(see page 136)*, and place Béthune, with its pavement brasseries, were largely rebuilt in the 1920s and 1930s after World War I. There are many examples of art deco style in Cubist wrought-iron balconies, angular corners and mosaic motifs.

Place de la République and 19th-Century Lille

Place de la République epitomises the grandiose vision of 19th-century French town planning: government at one end, culture at the other, and broad new boulevards offering perspectives to squares, churches and theatres in every direction. At one end of the square, the Préfecture du Nord – home to the Préfet, representing the central state administration – was built in 1863 by Charles Marteau, with a central

Plan Reliefs, Palais des Beaux-Arts

One of the curiosities of the Palais des Beaux-Arts is its collection, displayed in the basement, of 15 giant relief models of the towns fortified for Louis XIV by his military engineer Vauban, along what is now either side of the Franco-Belgian frontier. The making of reliefs was begun in the 17th century by Vauban and continued into the 19th century. More than simply models, they played a role in military strategy, revealing the importance of siege warfare at the time. At 1/600th scale, the detailed renditions of topography, buildings and Vauban's characteristic star-shaped fortifications are like historical snapshots of the different towns, including Calais, Charleroi, Namur, Ypres and a particularly elaborate model of Audenarde.

Old and new at the Palais des Beaux-Arts

pavilion inspired by the Louvre. At the other end of the square is the Palais des Beaux-Arts.

Palais des Beaux-Arts

The massive **Palais des Beaux-Arts** (open Mon 2–6pm, Wed–Sun 10am–6pm), Lille's fine-arts museum, is generally considered to be second only to the Louvre in France. The museum was fully refurbished in the 1990s, allowing many items to be brought out of the reserves and adding a glass-walled modern extension (by Jean-Marc Ibos and Myrto Vitart), which contains a restaurant and temporary exhibition galleries.

Unsurprisingly, the collection, in part built up from paintings seized from churches and convents after the French Revolution, is particularly strong in Flemish art, reflecting the Flemish artists who worked in Lille in the past. Highlights include Rubens' *Descent from the Cross*, painted for the Eglise des Capucines in Lille in 1616–17, and its preparatory oil sketch, and

La Lettre *(The Letter)*, *c.*1814–19 by Goya

his *Martyrdom of St Catherine*, as well as paintings by his pupils Van Dyck and Jordaens. Flemish mannerists include Maerten van Heemskerck, Brueghel the Younger and an elaborate *Allegory of the Vanities of the World* by Pieter Brel (1663). Fine Dutch paintings include *The Cornfield*, by Jacob van Ruisdael, Pieter Codde's melancholic young man and an interior by Pieter de Hooch.

The museum's two most arresting works, however, are probably the two paintings by Goya. ***Les Vieilles*** (The Old Women) is an extraordinary vision of old age and surely a morality tale. A gummy old lady in lacy white and her veiled black-dressed companion with rotting teeth sit beneath the looming, winged figure of Old Father Time. ***La Lettre*** (The Letter) presents a lighter, more frivolous image of two young women and a dog, promenading under a parasol against a sketchily rendered Madrid, and reading a love letter. The solidity, volume, joy and hope of youth contrast with the almost vanishing flesh and trembling fear of old age.

French paintings include David's *Belissarius Begging for Alms*, Delacroix's *Furious Medea* and Courbet's *After Dinner at Ornans*. The Impressionist and modern collection is small and patchy but does include Monet's *Houses of Parliament*, a portrait of Berthe Morisot by Manet and works by

Toulouse-Lautrec, Van Gogh and Léger. Among the Italian works, don't miss four roundels by Venetian master Veronese, as well as his *Paradise*, a preparatory study for a never-executed work for the Doge's Palace in Venice.

On the ground floor, the 19th-century sculpture includes work by Carpeaux, Frémiet and Rodin. There's also a representative survey of ceramics, including Chinese and Japanese porcelain, Italian maiolica, Dutch and local faïence, and porcelain from Lille, St-Omer, Arras and Valenciennes.

The medieval and Renaissance collection in the basement should not be overlooked either. Among its treasures are Douai artist Jean de Bellegambe's *Le Bain Mystique* triptyque, Donatello's subtle marble relief *Le Festin d'Herode*, illustrating his mastery of classical perspective, and the Dirk Bouts diptych of the *Ascent of the Elect* and *Fall of the Damned.* Needless to say, hell, with its swarming mass of nude doomed figures and many-eyed tailed beasts, gets a far more graphic representation than the tame joys of heaven.

Around Rue Solférino

Going north from the Préfecture towards the Citadelle, broad **boulevard de la Liberté**, laid out on the line of the former city ramparts, contains several imposing townhouses built in the 19th century by the city's industrial barons. On parallel rue de Solférino, the **Théâtre de Sébastopol** was built in 1903 in only 100 days in the eclectic style of the time – a touch of Byzantine here, coloured tiles there, and classical Atlantes propping up the door – and has served ever since for popular theatre and musicals. There's a street market on place Sébastopol on Wednesday and Saturday mornings.

Further along rue Solférino, the 19th-century former central covered market now houses a supermarket, but the surrounding streets, especially rue Masséna, are particularly lively at night, with studenty bars and restaurants.

Light sculpture by Sakis, Palais Rameau

Nineteenth-century Lille continues along boulevard Vauban. At No. 39 is the grand **Palais Rameau**, which began life in 1879 as a hall for horticultural exhibitions; it is half palace at the front and half greenhouse, in the form of a light-filled octagonal palm house, at the rear.

North of here, opposite the Citadelle, is the Jardin Vauban; to the south are the buildings of the Université Catholique, laid out in the 1880s around courtyards, inspired by Oxbridge colleges.

South of place de la République the perspective leads to the neo-Byzantine Eglise St-Michel. Just off place Philippe Le Bon, the **Maison Coilliot** (14 rue de Fleurus) is a flamboyant masterpiece of art nouveau architecture, designed in 1898–1900 by architect Hector Guimard for a local tile manufacturer – Coilliot's own mottled greeny-blue enamelled tiles cover the façade. Just beyond place Jeanne d'Arc, with the inevitable equestrian statue of the maid of Orleans, the **Musée d'Histoire Naturelle** (rue de Bruxelles; open Mon, Wed–Fri 9am–noon, 2–5pm, Sun 10am–1pm, 2–6pm) is an old-fashioned natural history museum in a grand 19th-century iron-framed structure. As well as all the requisite skeletons and stuffed animals and birds, it has a collection of plant fossils discovered in the region's mines, minerals, an ethnographic collection and items relating to the region's industrial past.

Broad **boulevard Jean-Baptiste Lebas** is full of imposing late 19th-century bourgeois houses. After decades as a scruffy parking lot, the square in the middle, which is a focus for antiques dealers during the Braderie de Lille every September, has recently been landscaped as a public park.

WAZEMMES

Southwest of place de la République, **Wazemmes** gives a taste of a multi-racial, working-class side of Lille. For the tourist, it's not so much a case of sights to be seen as an atmosphere to be absorbed, especially at the Sunday morning market. One of five ancient villages absorbed into Lille in 1858, Wazemmes is nowadays a cosmopolitan mix of the renovated and near-derelict, sprinkled with corner bars and African and North African restaurants. At the heart of the area are busy rue Léon Gambetta and the covered food market, a 19th-century brick-and-cast-iron structure (open Tues–Sun). On Sunday morning (and to a lesser extent Tuesday and

Trading in vegetables at Wazemmes covered food market

For the Maison Folie de Wazemmes, Dutch architect Lars Spuybroek restored the factory's brick architecture, created an outdoor street to link it to the surrounding district, and added an undulating computer-designed extension, clad in a dense steel mesh.

Thursday mornings), a huge **market** takes over the surrounding place de la Nouvelle Aventure and nearby streets; most of the shops along rue Léon Gambetta are also open. As well as fresh fruit, vegetables, flowers, *fringues* (cheap clothes), junk, bric-a-brac, household goods and live animals, you'll find stalls selling various tasty ethnic snacks. A local institution is the Bazar de Wazemmes (350 rue Léon Gambetta), an emporium for household china, kitchen equipment and porcelain.

On rue des Sarrazins, the transformation of the former Usine Leclerq textile factory into the **Maison Folie de Wazemmes** *(see pages 10 and 12)* has given the district a multi-disciplinary cultural centre, which aims to involve local residents, and is the most architecturally adventurous of the Maisons Folies created for Lille 2004. It is used for art and photography shows, cabaret, theatre and live music as well as harbouring artists' studios, a hammam and a café-brasserie.

MOULINS

Like Wazemmes, the district of **Moulins**, between St-Sauveur, the ring road and Wazemmes, was absorbed into the city in 1858. As the name suggests, countless mills once flourished here, though often not for grinding flour but for semi-industrial uses such as wood-sawing and oil pressing to make soaps and mastics. In the late 19th and early 20th centuries, Moulins was a centre of the textile industry, and huge red-brick factories were built amid the houses and workshops. Today, a large student population is breathing new life into the area, where converted industrial buildings coexist with recent public housing, and even some ancient rows of one-storey cottages that hark back to a more rural past.

Near the Porte de Douai Métro station (between rue de Douai, rue de Mulhouse and allée de la Filature), the **Filature**, a former linen-spinning plant converted by Reichen and Robert in 1975–81, is considered an exemplary piece of industrial rehabilitation. The immense red-brick building was converted into offices, flats, a crêperie, public library and Le Prato theatre, preserving not only the long red-brick façade and tall chimney, but also some internal iron columns and occasional bits of machinery. Across the street on rue de Fontenay, another refurbished factory houses the university law faculty.

Nearby, at 47 rue d'Arras, the **Brasserie des Trois-Moulins** is a derelict historic brewery that has been converted into a Maison Folie, where you can find exhibitions, live music and a bar/club, though the stables from the original 18th-century brewery still lie in semi-ruin.

On the other side of the ring road, the **Jardin des Plantes** (Botanical Garden; open May to Sept 7.30am–9pm, Oct to Apr 8.30am–6pm) offers some welcome breathing space. Trees are planted by continent, and there's a rose garden and a steamy tropical greenhouse.

The Jardin des Plantes

Centre Commercial Euralille

EURALILLE

Euralille is a 'laboratory of contemporary architecture', according to former prime minister and president of Lille Métropole, Pierre Mauroy. Unlike many modern business and commercial districts, which occupy former industrial outskirts of cities, Lille's Euralille development is plum next to Vieux Lille and the old Gare Lille Flandres. Its central location is one reason why this ambitious project, begun in the 1990s, seems to have been quickly adopted as part of the city. It uses land left empty by the demolition of old fortifications but criss-crossed by ring roads, railway tracks, the Métro line and tramway. At its heart is the glass-and-steel **Gare Lille Europe** TGV train station, symbolising former mayor Pierre Mauroy's vision of modernity and, like the Euralille name itself, Lille's position at the crossroads between France, Belgium and Great Britain.

Masterplanner Dutch architect and urbanist Rem Koolhaas brought in internationally renowned French architects including Christian de Portzamparc and Jean Nouvel. While the planning is resolutely modern, it also remains, largely, on a human scale, though head out of the station the wrong way and you can soon find yourself lost in a confusing mass of terraces and flyovers. The two most noticeable landmarks are the two towers that bridge the station: the striking L-shaped **Crédit Lyonnais office building** by Christian de Portzamparc, nicknamed 'the skiboot' or 'the pinball machine', and the 25-storey Lilleurope tower by Claude Vasconi. In front of them on avenue Le Corbusier is the long swooping Centre Commercial

Euralille shopping centre designed by Jean Nouvel, home to a huge Carrefour supermarket and a plethora of clothing and shoe chainstores, and topped by a colourful wall of four mini 'tower-ettes', containing offices, apartments and hotels.

Landscaping is still underway in the **Parc Henri Matisse**, laid out by garden designer Gilles Clément as a 'garden in motion', a grassy esplanade that connects the historic Porte de Roubaix to the TGV station and the copper-covered Cité des Affaires, containing offices, business centre and Crowne Plaza hotel. Koolhaas designed the **Lille Grand Palais**, a colossal oval conference centre, trade fair exhibition hall and auditorium. Currently rather isolated from the rest of Euralille, it will be joined by Euralille 2, a vast second phase extending alongside the St-Sauveur district; begun in 2004, it is due to continue until 2008, creating an area of housing in what urbanists Dusapin and Leclerq are describing as 'an inhabited wood'.

Christian de Portzamparc's Crédit Lyonnais building

Outdoor sculpture at the Musée d'Art Moderne Lille-Métropole

VILLENEUVE D'ASCQ

A drawn-out territory of landscaped university faculties, science park, low-rise housing and rural remains, the garden city of **Villeneuve d'Ascq** was created in 1970 out of the three villages of Flers, Annappes and Ascq; today, it is home to 67,000 residents and over 50,000 students. Modern developments, punctuated by a sprinkling of old village churches and farm buildings, are connected by landscaped parks and a string of artificial lakes created to drain the flood-prone land. The main sights are concentrated around three principal poles: the Parc Urbain, home to the internationally renowned modern art museum, and its eastward extension, the Parc du Héron, a lake and bird reserve; the Château de Flers; and, further south, the Hôtel de Ville.

Sitting in the midst of the Parc Urbain, within a landscaped sculpture park, is the **Musée d'Art Moderne Lille-Métropole** (1 allée du Musée; closed until early 2008; <www.mamlm.fr>). The low-slung red-brick-and-glass building by Roland Simounet opened in 1983, with a collection based on a fabulous donation by local industrialists Jean and Geneviève Masurel; it is particularly strong on the Fauves, Cubists and the work of the Ecole de Paris, including several Picassos, Modiglianis, Braques, Mirós and Légers, plus works by Roualt, Laurens, Kandinsky and Van Dongen. More recent contemporary acquisitions include works by Daniel Buren, Thomas Hirschhorn, Bernard Frize and Rirkrit Tiravanija. The museum is currently closed for the construction of an extension by architect Manuelle Gautrand to house an important collection of Art Brut – art produced by outsiders, often self-taught or in mental hospitals – and is due to reopen in early 2008.

The park continues through the watery Parc du Héron with its bird reserve and the **Asnapio** project (Parc Archéologique, rue Carpeaux, Quartier Cousinerie; open May–Oct Wed 2–5pm, Sun 3–7pm, Tues–Fri 2–5pm during school hols; tel: 03 20 47 21 99; <http://asnapio.villeneuvedascq.fr>), a recreation of Neolithic, Bronze Age, Iron Age, Roman and medieval dwellings based on archaeological sites in northern Europe.

Nearby, the **Musée des Moulins** (Mill Museum; rue Albert Samain; open Mon–Fri 10am–noon, 2–5pm, closed Aug and 15 Dec–15 Jan) gives a sense of the region's rural past. Two picturesque post mills and a water mill have been transported here and reconstructed piece by piece, reflecting a feature that was once so important in Flanders. There is also a small museum that explains milling techniques and uses, with a collection of stone mill wheels, including domestic ones dating from Roman times, sieving machines for cleaning grain, and mill mechanisms.

Musée des Moulins

The former village of Flers is distinguished by its Gothic church and the **Château de Flers** (chemin du Chat Botté), an intimate 17th-century château with stepped

The Mémorial d'Ascq 1944 (77 rue Mangin, Ascq, open Wed and Sun 2.30–5.30pm, July–Aug also open Tues and Thur) remembers a very dark moment in local history when in April 1944, 86 villagers were killed by an SS convoy arriving from the Russian front.

gables (now home to the tourist office, open Tues–Fri 9am–12.30pm, 2–6pm; Sat 9am–noon). In the cellars you can visit the **Musée du Château de Flers** (open Tues–Fri 2.30–5.30pm, first and third Sun of the month 2.30–5.30pm), where temporary exhibitions on archaeology and history are shown.

Nearby, the **Ferme d'en Haut** (238 rue Jules Guesde; exhibitions Wed, Sat, Sun 3–7pm) is an early 18th-century farm in stripy red brick and white stone, built around a large central courtyard. Containing artists' studios and a gallery, the farm has been extended and renovated to add a performance space, café, rehearsal room and restaurant.

At Annappes, another old farm contains the **Musée du Terroir** (open Mar–Nov Mon–Fri 2.30–5pm, Sun 3.30–6pm), consisting of reconstructed rural interiors, school, local crafts and an *estaminet* (inn) serving local specialities as well as a collection of traditional games.

Further south around the modern Hôtel de Ville is the **Forum des Sciences Centre François Mitterrand** (1 place de l'Hôtel de Ville; open Tues–Fri 10am–5.30pm, Sat–Sun 2–6.30pm), opened in 1996 to make science accessible to the general public. There's a planetarium, a themed exhibition that changes twice a year and an interactive section for children.

To the east, at 143 rue Colbert, is the **Musée du Plein Air** (open Apr–Oct Tues–Fri 10am–5pm, Sat–Sun 2.30–6pm). Twenty-two buildings representative of the rural architecture of northern France, including farms and chapels, have been reconstructed, to preserve architectural heritage and explain former rural traditions and crafts.

ROUBAIX

Quieter and visibly poorer than central Lille, **Roubaix** has been put on the tourist map by its art gallery, the fabulous La Piscine, Musée d'Art et d'Industrie *(see page 60)*. There are plenty of other reasons, too, why this 19th-century textile capital, designated a 'ville d'art et d'histoire' merits a visit in its own right, with its forward-thinking policy of industrial rehabilitation and an alternative arts scene. The monuments here are not historic mansions but red-brick factories with towering chimneys, many of them now seeing new life, whether as offices, dance studios, schools or shopping centres.

The town's association with textiles goes back to 1469 when Charles le Téméraire issued a charter granting Roubaix the permission to produce woollen cloth – a right previously reserved for Lille – but it was the arrival of steam power in

The Hôtel de Ville, Roubaix

Allo Visit is a mobile phone guide (tel: 08 92 68 25 11 + code 010 000) that allows you to discover Roubaix at your own pace on a pedestrian circuit. The commentary (in English or French) is accompanied by historic quotations, dramatised scenes and anecdotes, about the city's sights and sagas and the industrialists who made the city's wealth.

the early 19th century that saw weaving move from the farmhouse to the factory, and the town transformed from a semi-rural settlement to the fastest-growing urban area in France. The population soared from around 8,000 in 1800 to 35,000 in 1850 and 125,000 in 1900, as rural people who migrated to the city were joined by immigrants from across Flanders and Europe, and subsequently the Maghreb. Despite the decline of the textile industry in France, Roubaix continues to produce specialist luxury and high-tech fabrics and also has an outpost of the respected fashion design school ESMOD.

Grande Place

On one side of the **Grande Place**, Roubaix's **Hôtel de Ville**, built in 1911, is an elaborate neo-Renaissance confection that speaks of the confidence of the town's industrialists in the period leading up to World War I. It was designed by Victor Laloux, better known for the Gare d'Orsay (now Musée d'Orsay) in Paris. Along the cornice, admire the sculpted frieze, which illustrates the different stages of cloth production from sheep shearing via shipping to spinning and weaving. Inside you can see the grand staircase. One of the side pavilions is now the **Espace Croisé**, used for temporary art exhibitions.

Across the square, the neo-Gothic church of **St-Martin** follows the Flemish *hallekerke* model – like St-Maurice in Lille – with an almost square plan of five equal naves. The oldest building in Roubaix, it was remodelled from 1849 to 1852 to meet the needs of the soaring population, though some of the old monuments remain; these include the medieval tombs of François de Luxembourg and Isabeau de Roubaix, and an elaborate, carved-and-gilded, 16th-century wooden altarpiece depicting the life of St John the Baptist in three-dimensional scenes. Outside, the belfry dates from 1511. Nearby, with façades painted in cheerful colours, place de la Liberté is home to cafés and the tourist office (10 rue de la Tuilerie).

From the Grande Place, leading towards the fanciful 19th-century railway station, **avenue Jean-Baptiste Lebas** is lined with an array of banks, former textile companies' head-quarters and the late 19th-century Grand Hôtel. The most elaborate building of all is the ENSAIT (Ecole Nationale Supérieure des Arts et Industries de la Textile), a textile research institute on place des Martyrs.

Colourful houses on avenue Jean-Baptiste Lebas

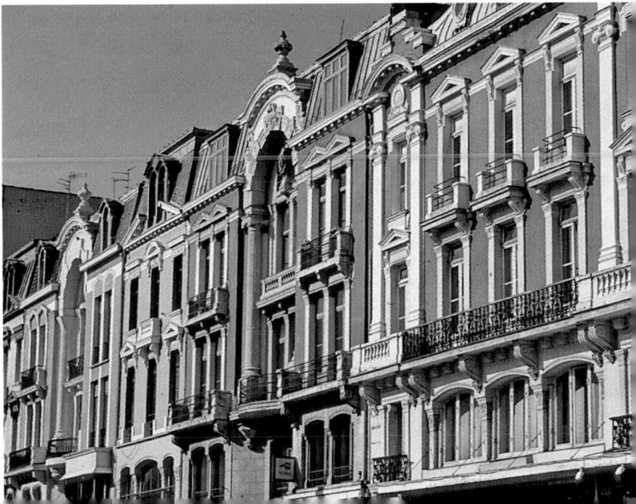

La Piscine

Close by, **La Piscine, Musée d'Art et d'Industrie** (23 rue de l'Espérance; open Tues–Thur 11am–6pm, Fri 11am–8pm, Sat, Sun 1–6pm) is as much as an attraction for its setting in a brilliantly converted art deco swimming pool, as for its collection of ceramics, textiles and fine art. The pool, in use until 1984, was built between 1927 and 1932 'for the workers' by the socialist council, as an expression of new ideas about hygiene and healthy exercise. Architect Jean-Paul Phillipon created a new entrance in the shell of the adjacent former textile factory, but preserved the swimming pool layout, with its art deco stained-glass sunburst, and wave motifs on mosaics and

friezes; water still gushes out of Neptune's mouth at one end, and there's even a strip of water down the centre, on either side of which stand 19th-century sculptures. Around the pool, two floors of tiled changing cabins now display ceramics, including Picasso vases, art deco designs from Sèvres and an array of textile samples and designs, from Coptic fragments and 18th-century silk to clothes by contemporary designers such as Jean-Charles de Castelbajac and Yoji Yamamoto.

Displayed in galleries around the sides, the fine-art collection focuses on 19th- and early 20th-century French paintings. It includes Ingres' nude *Angélique*, Orientalist works by Gérôme and Bernard, an oil sketch of lions by Rosa Bonheur, and *La Petite Châtelaine*, the bust of a little girl hollowed out of a block of marble by Camille Claudel. The sculpture is almost translucent and has a youthful innocence that is distinct from many of Claudel's more anguished works. The most celebrated piece in the collection is probably *The Cock Fight*, painted by local artist Rémy Cogghe, capturing the tension and excitement as the crowd eggs on the combatants in a sport that was still popular in the north when painted in 1889.

The 20th-century collection is strong on the Modernist figuration of the Ecole de Paris (Pascin, Foujita and da Lempicka) and works by the Groupe de Roubaix of the 1950s, notably Eugène Leroy.

La Piscine, Roubaix

South of the Grande Place, rue du Maréchal Foch leads to the broad boulevard Charles de Gaulle in one direction and boulevard du Général Leclerc in the other, with the tramway running down the centre. Both are lined with the eclectically styled houses put up for textile barons and the wealthy bourgeoisie. Look out for a rare example of art nouveau at No. 16, a house built on the model of a Renaissance hospice; it is now the ESMOD fashion design school. In addition, note the Rang des Drapiers, a terrace of ornate neo-Flemish houses at 52–88 boulevard Charles de Gaulle. A leaflet available at the tourist office picks out the most interesting buildings.

Parc Barbieux

At the southern end of boulevard Charles de Gaulle is **Parc Barbieux**, laid out in 1878 by Georges Hautmont and probably the finest park in the Lille Métropole. The park came

Roubaix's verdant Parc Barbieux

about through something of a planning disaster: originally a section of the canal between Lille and the Belgian frontier was to be dug along here, but the project was abandoned. The flood-prone land could not be built on, so in a face-saving change of plan it was turned into this spacious park instead.

Factory Heritage

At 78 boulevard du Général Leclerc, the 19th-century Motte-Bossut spinning factory looks more like a medieval castle than a dark satanic mill, with its crenellated façade and tall red-brick turret. It was brilliantly renovated in the 1990s by Alain Sarfati, who created a galleried central space inside and added a high-tech steel drawbridge over the entrance. It now houses the **Archives du Monde du Travail** (open for exhibitions Mon–Fri 1–6pm), part of the French state archives, and is used for temporary exhibitions relating to industry and the workplace. Other rehabilitated industrial premises can be seen on rue des Arts, where one factory is now the dance studio of Ballet du Nord, and, at No. 69, a former clothing workshop (open Sat 3–7pm) cheerfully claims to be 'La Plus Petite Galerie du Monde (ou Presque)' – 'the smallest gallery in the world (or almost)' – and puts on regular exhibitions of contemporary art.

Weavers themselves give the tours at the **Manufacture des Flandres – Musée du Jacquard** (25 impasse de la Prudence; open Tues–Sat and some Sun 1.30–6pm), a working factory where you can see textiles being woven on a variety of looms from antique wooden examples to modern high-tech ones, by a company that specialises in patterned Jacquard weaves and reproductions of ancient tapestries.

Roubaix's latest attraction is **La Condition Publique** (place du Général Faidherbe, <www.laconditionpublique.com>), in the rehabilitated 1901 Le Conditionnement Public complex, where wool was 'conditioned', weighed, analysed and stored to ensure that its weight and humidity remained constant.

Behind a polychrome brick façade, the huge expanse of buildings has been converted into an art gallery (open during exhibitions, usually Tues–Sat 12.30–6.30pm), concert and performance space, studios for artists-in-residence, bookshop, a gallery relating to Roubaix's architectural heritage, and a funky bar and restaurant. Even more unusual is the experimental garden on the roof: the 'soil' here has been formed out of the dust, dirt and pollution carried up on to the roof over the years in a type of natural colonisation of the urban environment, by seedlings carried by wind or seeds that have arrived in bales of wool from as far away as Australia.

A few streets away, in an area of brick terraced workers' housing, is the Canal de Roubaix. With its locks and bridges, the canal reveals a positively bucolic aspect of Roubaix.

The other reason many people visit Roubaix is for its factory shop outlets, where the previous season's stock, mainly clothes

La Condition Publique, a major addition to Roubaix's cultural scene

and shoes, is sold at discount prices. There are two complexes: MacArthur Glen (mail de Lannoy), purpose-built around a twee little street in the centre of town, and **L'Usine**, a 1903 factory where velvet was formerly manufactured, at 228 avenue Alfred Motte *(see page 93)*.

L'Usine, now a factory shop

Other Highlights

Between Lille and Roubaix are two masterpieces of 20th-century architecture. At Croix stands the **Villa Cavrois** (60 avenue J.F. Kennedy), designed by architect Robert Mallet-Stevens in 1931–2 for the industrialist Paul Cavrois. Sticking out amid the bourgeois villas, the long, low Cubist structure in reinforced concrete was avant-garde not only in its play of volumes, terraces and openings but also in its conception of a modern lifestyle, complete with lift, loudspeakers integrated into each room, and swimming pool, as well as furniture designed by the architect. It had fallen into a state of near dereliction after being sold by the family in 1986, but was bought by the Métropole in the late 1990s and will hopefully be restored.

At Hem, the **Chapelle Ste-Thérèse** (14 rue de Croix; visits by appointment; tel: 03 28 33 80 24), built 1956–8, was commissioned by the industrialist Philippe Leclerc. The simple, pared-back geometrical form by Swiss architect Hermann Baur sets off an altar by sculptor Dodeigne, a striking curvilinear mosaic over the porch by Jean Barillet and, above all, painter Alfred Manessier's magnificent stained glass – an abstract evocation of the life of St Teresa.

TOURCOING

Another textile city, **Tourcoing** almost joins on to Roubaix in the urban sprawl. It boomed in the 19th century when industrialists erected grand houses: the town hall was rebuilt like a pompous mini château, the church was enlarged, and new broad avenues were laid out connecting the town to Roubaix and Lille. The city has a worthwhile art museum and is also home to the respected Atelier Lyrique opera company, the Théâtre de l'Idéal (an outpost of Théâtre du Nord) and the innovative Le Fresnoy post-graduate art school.

The 1970s were not kind to Tourcoing – happily, there are plans to demolish the ugly bus station and multi-storey car park – but the centre of town is still the Grand' Place and its adjoining squares, the setting for a sprawling food and clothes market on Monday and Thursday mornings. On place Charles et

Musée des Beaux-Arts, Tourcoing

Albert Roussel, the **Chambre de Commerce**, built in Flemish neo-Renaissance style with belfry, today contains a local history centre (open Mon, Wed–Fri 9.30–11.30am, 2–5pm; Sat, Sun 2–6pm). **Eglise St-Christophe** (open May–Oct 1st and 3rd Sun of month 2–6pm, or by appointment; tel: 03 20 27 55 24), begun in the 13th century and extended in neo-Gothic style during the 19th-century industrial boom, has an impressive 62-bell carillon and a small museum relating to bell-ringing. It's a 220-step climb to the top of the tower, but once there you are rewarded with the bell room, dial room, bell-ringer's cabin and a fine view.

Tourcoing's impressive World War I memorial (above), on place de la Victoire, crowns the entrance to the town from Roubaix. Sculpted in white stone by Lucien Brasseur in 1924–31, it is an unusually dynamic monument, as figures of the fallen climb in pyramid formation behind a figure of Victory on a winged horse.

Near to the Hôtel de Ville, the **Musée des Beaux-Arts de Tourcoing** (2 rue Paul Doumer; open Mon, Wed–Sun 1.30–6pm) occupies the former house of composer Albert Roussel, and its spacious, purpose-built 1930s' extension by Henri and Jean Maillard. Tourcoing's fine-art museum has an adventurous policy of juxtaposing old masters with modern and contemporary art to try to show the influences and inspirations of many contemporary works, and the astonishingly similar concerns, or 'modernity' of ideas, in many historic ones. Thus a 1950s', near-abstract landscape in the typical

Fountain in Tourcoing

thick paint of Tourcoing-born Eugène Leroy hangs next to a 17th-century Flemish mannerist landscape by Tobias Van Haecht; and an 18th-century still life may be displayed alongside a modern sculpture. Other highlights include Jean-Louis Boilly's *Caricature Heads*, a wall drawing by Sol LeWitt in the prints and drawings gallery, and rooms devoted to Jean Fautrier and Swiss artist Markus Raetz.

The other highlight at Tourcoing is the **Hospice d'Havré** (100 rue de Tournai). Restored as a Maison Folie in 2004, for exhibitions, artists' residences, theatre, literature and music workshops and a library, it was founded, like the Hospice Comtesse in Vieux Lille, as a charity hospital, later becoming a convent and then serving as the municipal hospital until the 1990s. Today, it stands out as the best-preserved example of 17th- to 18th-century hospice architecture in the region, with its severe, almost unadorned, red-brick façades, built around a cloister, and its pitched-slate roofs. The 15th-century chapel has a 17th-century baroque altarpiece.

Behind the Hospice, on avenue Gustave Dron, the shopping street that connects the town centre to the railway station, take a look at **Les Arcades**, a long 1930s' apartment block with arcaded ground-floor shops and decorative brick-and-coloured-tile façades (less grandiose when seen from the Hospice side).

Another curiosity, though with very limited opening hours, is the **Musée du 5 juin 1944, Message Verlaine** (4 bis avenue de la Marne; open 1st and 3rd Sun of month, 9am–noon, 2–6pm, except July–Aug). Devoted to wartime radio technology, it is installed in the underground bunker (be prepared for chilly conditions) in which the German army first decoded the broadcast on Radio London announcing the D-Day landings.

Towards Roubaix, **Le Fresnoy Studio National des Arts Contemporains** (22 rue du Fresnoy; <www.le-fresnoy.tm.fr>) is an innovative postgraduate art school, equipped with sound and film studios and open to the public for art exhibitions and repertory cinema. The glass-and-steel structure, designed by Swiss architect Bernard Tschumi in 1997, was built around a former cinema, bowling alley and dance-hall complex.

OTHER PARTS OF LILLE METROPOLE

Lambersart

North of the Citadelle, the residential suburb of Lambersart is known for its fanciful 19th- and early 20th-century villas on tree-lined avenues, such as avenue de l'Hippodrome. Note the almost belfry-like turret of the Villa St-Charles at No. 183, winner of a prize for the most beautiful façade in 1895. In the 1880s, Lambersart became a pleasure area for the Lillois with its racetrack and popular *guinguette* (dance hall). A recent addition is the **Colysée**, a modern glass-and-wood construction beside the Deûle on the site of the old *guinguette*, which is now used for exhibitions.

Marcq-en-Barœul and Bondues

The smart residential areas of **Marcq-en-Barœul** and **Bondues** reveal a more rural aspect of the conurbation, with historic châteaux and swathes of arable land and pasture. As well as large bourgeois houses, often with huge gardens, around avenue de la République (the 'Nouveau Boulevard' that linked Lille to Tourcoing and Roubaix in the early 20th century), Marcq-en-Barœul is known for its **Hippodrome** (racetrack).

Running across the two communes is the 60-hectare (150-acre) **Parc du Septentrion**, a favourite local promenade, with pools, formal gardens and a landscaped *parc à l'anglaise*, partially laid out by garden designer Russell Page in the 1930s. There is also a growing outdoor sculpture trail, which includes works by local artists Dodeigne and Paul Hémery and 16th-century sculptor Giambologna, who, although more usually associated with Florence and Italian mannerism, was actually born in Douai. In the park is the moated **Château du Vert-Bois** (visits Sun 3.30pm and 5pm), an elegant 18th-century residence built on the site of a fortified farm. On the edge of the park, the Village Artisanal is home to a cluster of carpenters, potters and other craftspeople.

The Distillerie de Wambrechies

Wambrechies

Around 7km (4 miles) north of Lille, **Wambrechies** is a pretty canalside community. Its chief attraction is the fascinating tour of the **Distillerie de Wambrechies** (1 rue de la Distillerie; open daily but reserve three days ahead, tel: 03 20 14 91 91). In this listed monument, with its original 19th-century buildings, *genièvre (see box)* is still made on historic machines using the traditional method developed by the Claeyssens family and their engineer Henri Lenssen. The waterside mill was bought by Guillaume Claeyssens in 1789 for manufacturing linen cloth, then converted into a mill for pressing linseed oil, before his son turned it into a far more profitable distillery in 1817. Production at the start of the 20th century (when the factory employed 60 workers) was 10 times what it is today, although there has been a something of a revival because of recent renewed interest in local traditions.

***Ginièvre*, once the favourite drink of miners and factory workers, is a spirit made from rye and malt barley. Like gin, it is flavoured with juniper, but its taste is closer to that of whisky.**

The tour takes you through the different stages of production, and there's a chance to taste – and buy – at the end. Manufacture stops from May to August because of the heat, and for the cleaning and upkeep of the machines. You can also take boat trips to the distillery from Lille along the Deûle.

Seclin

Southwest of Lille, sprawling **Seclin** has some notable historic monuments. The 13th-century **Collégiale St-Piat**, with its ring of chapels around the choir, baroque altar and crypt, is much grander inside than the exterior suggests. On the edge of the town, the **Hospice de Seclin** (rue des Marronniers), established by Marguerite de Flandres, is another great medieval charitable foundation, that remains a hospital today, with beautifully preserved 17th-century brick architecture built around an arcaded courtyard (for both, book a week ahead, tel: 03 20 90 12 12). The extravagant **Domaine Mandarine Napoléon** (open Tues–Sat 10am–5.30pm; <www.domainenapoleon.com>), combines a distillery for the liqueur much loved by Napoleon and a collection of artefacts connected with the great man himself.

BORDER HOPPING

Courtrai (Kortrijk)

Only minutes from Lille is Flemish-speaking Belgium. The town of **Courtrai** or Kortrijk (signposts are in both French and Flemish) dates to Roman times, but it is the Middle Ages that are more evident. The imposing **Broel towers** are remnants of medieval fortifications on either side of the Pont de Broel, which leads to the Buda island, and are now something of a cultural focus. The **Broelmuseum** (open Tues–Sun 10am–noon, 2–5pm, closed Christmas to New Year), a fine and decorative arts museum, has a good collection of Flemish paintings, including works by Roeland Savery and other artists who worked in Courtrai, and an important collection of ceramics.

Back across the river are the Gothic-Renaissance town hall and the Gothic belfry, once part of the medieval drapers' mar-

Broel towers, Courtrai

ket, which dominates the Grote Markt, the main square. Nearby is the tranquil 17th-century *béguinage* or *begijnhof*, now UNESCO-listed. This all-female lay community, established in the Middle Ages, is a veritable little town within a town, with small houses sited around two squares. One house, the Maison de la Grande-Dame, is now a small museum (open Wed–Mon 10am–noon, 2–5pm). At the other side of the *béguinage*, the cloister of the **Abbaye de Groeninge** (Groeningheabjdij) contains a museum of local history (open daily 10am–noon, 2–5pm), giving pride of place to the Battle of the Golden Spurs – or Battle of Courtrai – a celebrated victory of Flemish troops over the French king in 1302.

Tournai

Tournai was another great wool town that, like Lille, oscillated over the centuries between French and Flemish rule. A Merovingian capital and important medieval bishopric, it has a rich architectural heritage of medieval houses and churches, 19th-century industrial buildings and patricians' residences – and even a cluster of art nouveau houses around the railway station – despite much reconstruction after World War I.

The extraordinary silhouette of the vast Romanesque and Gothic **Cathédrale** (open daily) on place de l'Evêché dominates the town, thanks to its five square towers, but several other medieval churches also contribute to the town's nickname: 'the town with one hundred bell towers'. Nearby, on the Grande Place, are the **belfry** (open Tues–Sat and Sun afternoon) – the oldest in Belgium – begun in 1188 but later doubled in height, and the beautiful Renaissance **Halle aux Draps** (Drapers' Hall). The other side of the belfry, place Reine-Astrid was laid out as part of the neoclassical embellishments of the French empire in the early 19th century, with its striking circular concert hall and the **Hôtel Gorin**, now a museum devoted to the tapestries for which the town was once famed.

EXCURSIONS

Gabled houses in Arras

Arras

Although much of **Arras** was flattened in World War I, its two remarkable arcaded squares, the **Grand' Place** and the **Place des Héros** have survived – or have been beautifully reconstructed – with their narrow gabled houses, busy with shops and restaurants, as have the 16th-century town hall and belfry. A five-minute walk from place des Héros, the **Musée des Beaux-Arts** (22 rue Paul Doumer; open Wed–Mon 9.30am–noon and 2–5.30pm) is housed in the elegant 18th-century buildings of the former Abbaye St-Vaast. The collection of medieval religious art includes fine tombstones, statues and Gothic altarpieces, and there are paintings by Jean de Bellegambe, Philippe de Champaigne, Corot and Rousseau, as well as blue-and-white Arras-ware, porcelain from Tournai and archaeological finds – including traces of Roman Nemetacum.

At the far side of the abbey buildings is the imposing neoclassical Cathédrale St-Vaast. Near the theatre in the network of old streets around the abbey, the 18th-century **Hôtel de Guines** (rue des Jongleurs) has been rehabilitated as a Maison Folie for exhibitions, chamber concerts and small-scale theatre and cabaret. More unexpected are the town's labyrinthine subterranean passages, which have existed since the Middle Ages and were used by British soldiers during World War I; they can be visited in tours organised by the office de tourisme (in the town hall). There's also a British war cemetery in the town *(see box opposite)*.

Boulogne-sur-Mer

Today a busy fishing port and tourist resort on the Côte Opale, **Boulogne-sur-Mer** is an historic town with plenty of charm. Its hilly site made it a natural strategic point both for defence and for those who wanted to invade England, from the ancient Romans to Napoleon and Hitler. The town is divided into two parts, the old upper town or Haute Ville and the modern lower town. The Haute Ville is still surrounded by its medieval city wall, broken only by four fortified gateways. The skyline is

World War I Battlefields

World War I not only decimated the male population of Europe, but also transformed the landscape, as the front edged its way backwards and forwards often over the same small stretch of ground for years, with the opposing armies sometimes less than 100m (100yds) apart. In the flat landscape of Flanders, the Artois and the Somme, even a tiny ridge took on an enormous tactical importance. Whole towns and villages were flattened and farms wiped out. While a few were rebuilt identically (as in Ypres in Belgium and the Grand' Place in Arras), even today it is very apparent in some areas that most of the buildings date from the 20th century. Hundreds of military cemeteries dot the countryside.

On the wooded ridge of Notre-Dame de Lorette, just north of Arras, is a moving French national monument and ossuary, with a cemetery of 20,000 named graves and eight ossuaries containing the remains of another 20,000 unknown French soldiers. Nearby, shell holes and bomb craters are still visible around Vimy ridge, where a memorial, surrounded by pine and maple trees, commemorates over 66,000 Canadians who died in World War I; British and French cemeteries are close by. At Arras, there is a British memorial, and the office de tourisme organises visits to the underground tunnels used by British troops. Further south, the excellent Historial de la Grande Guerre at Péronne looks at World War I from French, British and German perspectives.

dominated by the colonnaded double drum dome of the **Basilica Notre-Dame** (open Apr–Aug 9am–noon, 2–6pm; Sept–Mar 10am–noon, 2–5pm; crypt and treasury open Tues–Sat 2–5pm, Sun 2.30–5pm). Built in the 19th century over a much earlier crypt, this church was for centuries the focus of a pilgrimage cult that saw both French and English monarchs pay homage to 'Our Lady of the Sea', a miraculous statue of the Virgin, which was washed up on the shore in the 7th century.

Now lined with restaurants, the main street, rue de Lille, follows one of the original Roman thoroughfares. On **place de la Mairie** stands the town hall and adjoining stone belfry, the neoclassical Palais de Justice and the library, in a former convent. On one side of the old town, the 13th-century castle, with a ring of turrets around a central courtyard (the first castle to be built without a central keep), now contains **Le Château Musée** (open Mon and Wed–Sat 10am–12.30pm and 2–5pm, Sun 10am–12.30pm and 2.30–5.30pm), a municipal museum displaying local painting and pottery, Greek and Etruscan vases and, more surprisingly, a collection of Inuit sculpture and artefacts.

Boulogne's Haute Ville

Through the Porte des Dunes, the Grande Rue runs through the lower town towards the quayside, with its large commercial dock area and ferry port. Largely rebuilt in the 1950s, it is today France's largest fishing port and the biggest fish-processing centre in Europe, though there is also small-scale fishing with the catch sold every morning at stalls on quai Gambetta in front of the tourist office.

Admiring the fish at Nausicaa

At the start of Boulogne's long sandy beach (bathing is currently banned at the Boulogne end because of pollution), which stretches towards the seaside suburb of Wimereux, stands the modern aquarium **Nausicaa** (boulevard Ste-Beuve; open daily 9.30am–6.30pm, July and Aug till 7.30pm, closed 8–26 Jan 2007; <www.nausicaa.fr>), the most popular tourist attraction in the region. Both temperate and tropical marine species are on display here. The route around the spiky angular building involves lots of ups and downs as you move from deep-water shoals to the tidal zone and the pools of a tropical lagoon. An ecological angle on the future of fishing and how North Sea species survive pollution make it just as interesting for adults as for children. Highlights include sticking your head up among the colourful species of the tropical lagoon, the inverted pyramid in the tuna tank, the open-air sea lion pool and, of course, the sharks.

Just outside the town, ringed by imperial eagles and laurel wreaths and crowned by a statue of Napoleon, stands the 54-m (117-ft) high, white marble **Colonne de la Grande Armée**, which commemorates the army with which Napoleon planned to invade Great Britain from its encampment here in 1803–5. This abortive attempt at an invasion is celebrated in a festive costumed re-enactment each July.

Le Cateau-Cambrésis

Henri Matisse is usually associated with Nice and the French Riviera where he spent the end of his life, but he was born in 1869 in the small town of **Le Cateau-Cambrésis** in the north of France. His grandparents were weavers, and the colours and patterns of textiles – as well as the quality of light of northern France – remained a continual influence in his work. His attachment to the area is demonstrated in the 82 works he donated to his birthplace two years before his death; these form the basis of the **Musée Matisse** (open Wed–Mon 10am–6pm).

Treasures include early works from the 1890s, a superb Fauve-period *Portrait of Marguerite* from 1906, flowers painted in Morocco, interiors from the 1940s and the *Femme à la Gandara Rouge*, his last oil painting. Particularly moving is the restored plaster ceiling brought here from the Hôtel Régina in Nice. Depicting the heads of his grandchildren, it was painted

Artworks at the Musée Matisse

by the 80-year-old artist from his bed with a brush attached to a pole. The museum is housed in the pretty Palais Fenelon, the former summer residence of the bishops of Cambrai, evidence that this small town was once more important than it is today. An extension has enlarged the gallery space, as well as adding a café and temporary exhibition galleries. The museum also shows geometrical abstract paintings by Herbin and a rich collection of artists' books. A short walk away is the primary school where Matisse designed a stained-glass window known as *Les Abeilles* (The Bees), because the white bands that run in an arc across the geometric pattern resemble bees' wings.

Douai

One of the great former Flemish wool towns, along with Lille, Ghent, Bruges and Ypres, **Douai** was later an important iron-working town, which left it with a grim industrial reputation. The town reached its apogee in the Middle Ages and northern Renaissance. Housed in the buildings of a former monastery, the **Musée de la Chartreuse** (open Wed–Mon 10am–noon, 2–6pm) is a fine-art collection that reflects the town's rich cultural past. Of note is 16th-century master Jean de Bellegambe's *Polyptyque d'Anchin*, showing Christ sitting on a red-robed God on the heavenly throne. The law courts are housed in another former monastic building with Gothic arcades opening on to the River Scarpe. Next to the town hall, the 14th- to 15th-century **belfry** is one of the oldest in France, with a 62-bell carillon. There's a great view from the top (193 steps).

About 8km (5 miles) east of town is the **Centre Historique Minier de Lewarde** (open Mar–Oct daily 9am–5.30pm, Nov–Feb Mon–Sat 1–5pm and Sun 10am–5pm; closed Jan; <www.chm-lewarde.com>), a relic of the region's mining industry. Guided tours of the old mine conducted by former miners include a visit to the pit baths and a voyage in the mine train through mine shafts.

Playing boules on the plage des Allies, near Dunkerque

Dunkerque

Synonymous in British memory with the evacuation of troops during the early stages of World War II, **Dunkerque** (Dunkirk) – by the end of the 19th century, France's third busiest port – was so heavily damaged in the war that it is hard to imagine today what this historic port must have been like in its heyday. Yet the post-war reconstruction – mainly low-rise red brick – is not unpleasant: old warehouses and other relics point to Dunkerque's prestigious past, and the town has the undoubted ambience of a working port, as well as a notable port museum.

The town is renowned for its lively *Carnaval* at the start of Lent, when there are processions and herring-throwing festivities around town. In the town centre, the neo-Flemish town hall was built in 1901 by Louis-Marie Cordonnier (architect of the Opéra and Nouvelle Bourse in Lille); nearby is the large church of St-Eloi and its 15th-century belfry, while on the other side is the medieval Tour de Leughenaer, which probably served as a decoy lighthouse intended to send enemy ships on to the sandbanks.

On place du Général de Gaulle, the **Musée des Beaux-Arts** (open Wed–Mon 10am–12.15pm, 1.45–6pm) has a representative collection of French and northern art from the 16th–20th centuries, including a head by Van Dyck and a striking portrait of a young man by Hyacinthe Rigaud. Much more atmospheric, however, is the **Musée Portuaire** (quai de la Citadelle; open Sept–June Wed–Mon 10am–12.45pm,1.30–6pm; July–Aug daily 10am–6pm; <www.museeportuaire.com>), on the other side of the basin in a tobacco warehouse dating from 1869. Models and paintings of Vauban's fortifications, legendary corsair Jean Bart, ship models, paintings and vintage photographs tell the history of the port, which was first used for military purposes, and later important for cod fishing off Iceland and the export of textiles. The maritime museum puts the emphasis on port activities, such as piloting, dragging and customs. Moored outside are the three-masted *Duchesse Anne*, a barge, and a red lighthouse ship, the *Sandettie*. The first two vessels can be visited on tours as part of the museum. It is possible to follow a trail around the docks (leaflet available from the museum) or to take boat trips around the docks on *La Bazenne*.

Gravelines

On the banks of the River Aa, **Gravelines** is another walled Vauban town that doubles as a low-key seaside resort. Its perfectly preserved system of defences and waterways can be visited by boat, as can the bay, with its fortresses. On one side of the town is the Citadelle, where the powder room now contains a small museum devoted to prints and drawings. To the northeast of the old town is Gravelines beachside annexe, where beach huts, a children's play area and sand dunes all lie, rather surrealistically, in sight of France's largest nuclear power station, now the town's main employer.

Quaint street in Cassel

Les Monts de Flandres

Anywhere else, the **Monts de Flandres** would go unnoticed, but in flat Flanders, this peaceful hilly area can almost be described as mountainous. Nothing dramatic then, but these hills offer fine views over the surrounding lowlands. The peaceful countryside, dotted with windmills, brick houses, church spires and *estaminet* bars, is popular for walking and cycling.

A cobbled street winds up the hill to the top of **Cassel**, offering pretty views and a surprisingly impressive Grand' Place that runs along the ridge lined with *hôtels particuliers*, indicating its prosperous past. Maréchal Ferdinand Foch, commander of French forces in World War I, had his headquarters here, in what is now the smart Châtellerie de Schoebeque hotel. Look for the fine stone Renaissance façade of the Hôtel Lenglé and the 18th-century Hôtel d'Hallium, home to a cluster of antiques dealers. The tourist office is in another fine townhouse.

Below Cassel, on the scenic D948 route that leads to Steenvoorde, is the **Moulin de la Roome**, an historic wooden postmill; there's another mill on the edge of Steenvoorde, a small yet lively town with a Grande Place lined with bars, and another mill hugging the frontier at Boescheppe, where the nearby Mont des Cats – a high point at all of 158m (518ft) – is famed for the cheese made at the monastery.

Bergues and Hondschoote

Bergues has perfectly preserved star-shaped Vauban defences and moat, showing the system of ramparts and waterways that was so important to Louis XIV's defence of the north. Within the ramparts are neat terraces of brick houses. The 17th-century Mont de Piété contains the municipal museum (closed Tues); its chief treasure is a rare painting by 17th-century artist Georges de la Tour. On the canal, on the north side of town, the flower-decked *estaminet* (inn) Le Brueghel is also worth a look.

East of Bergues, reached by the D110, **Hondschoote** has a Renaissance town hall and a late Gothic brick church, Eglise St-Vaast, which has carved baroque retables and a fine organ loft. Just outside town, the Noordmeulen windmill, dating from 1127, is probably the oldest in Europe. As well as pasture and arable land, in summer you'll also see fields of blue flax flowers – some linen is still produced in the area, a tradition explained in a museum on the main square.

St-Omer

Perched on an escarpment above the River Aa and the Audomarois marshes, elegant **St-Omer** seems to have preserved its 18th-century calm. The vast Gothic cathedral, crowning the top of the hill, has a soaring nave and a *Descent from the Cross* by Rubens. Behind the cathedral the former bishop's palace is now the law courts. Housed in an 18th-century mansion, the **Musée de l'Hôtel Sandelin** (14 rue Carnot; open Wed–Sun 10am–noon, 2–6pm) displays period furniture and paintings plus an important collection of faïence and medieval artworks.

Also in St-Omer is the Musée Henri Dupuis (6 rue Henri Dupuis; open Wed–Sun 10am–noon and 2–6pm), a collection of stuffed birds, minerals, ceramics and objets d'art arranged like a 19th-century cabinet of curiosities.

EPICERIE
du Père Peinard
PAIN CUIT
- au -
FEU DE BOIS
RICE
KRISPIES

WHAT TO DO

A mixture of highly respected national institutions and more alternative local associations, combined with a long tradition of lively festivals, make up an arts scene to satisfy even the most-discerning culture vulture. Various free magazines, such as *Sortir* and *DDO L'Agenda*, available from the tourist office, bars or hotels, provide information on what's going on.

ENTERTAINMENT

Théâtre du Nord (<www.theatredunord.fr>), directed by American Stuart Seide, draws on a repertoire that ranges from Shakespeare and Molière to contemporary playwrights such as Howard Barker. The company, which also welcomes visiting theatre groups and directors, is based in a modern auditorium behind the historic Grand' Garde on the Grand' Place, and also performs at the Théâtre de l'Idéal in Tourcoing.

Lille Métropole is also home to some 30 other theatres and theatre companies. The ornate **Théâtre Sébastopol** has presented popular theatre and stand-up comedy since it opened in 1903. The **Rose des Vents** (<www.larosedesvents-scenenationale.com>) in Villeneuve d'Ascq focuses on contemporary playwrights and also programmes dance. It organises the Scènes Etrangères international dance and theatre festival in May. The **Théâtre du Prato** aims at popular physical theatre based on circus arts and clowning, and performs on stage at the Filature *(see page 51)*, under the big top and even on a barge. The **Théâtre de la Découverte** stages politically engaged plays at La Verrière, while the historic **Théâtre Louis Richard** marionette theatre in Roubaix puts on a programme that proves that puppets can be just as much for adults as for children.

Shop window on rue de la Monnaie

With the **Orchestre National de Lille** <www.onlille.com> Lille possesses one of the finest regional symphony orchestras in France. The orchestra has contributed greatly to the city's cultural reputation since it was founded in 1976, largely thanks to the dedication of conductor Jean-Claude Casadesus. Based at the Nouveau Siècle building in the centre of Lille, it also performs at the Opéra de Lille and elsewhere in the region, as well as touring. Casadesus' ambition to open up classical music to a wider audience has included concerts in such unusual venues as factories, a prison and a coal mine, just before it closed down. The **Atelier Lyrique de Tourcoing**, under director Jean-Claude Malgoire, is renowned for experimental opera productions. It performs mainly at the Théâtre Municipal in Tourcoing but also at the Opéra de Lille. It is best known for its baroque repertoire in collaboration with the Grande Ecurie et la Chambre du Roy orchestra, which performs on early instru-

Ballet du Nord rehearsals

ments, but it also presents classical opera and even contemporary pieces.

After several years of work, the lovely **Opéra de Lille** (<www.opera-lille.fr>) has been restored to its former glory, and is used for opera, classical concerts, ballet and contemporary dance. The **Ballet du Nord** (<www.balletdunord.com>) performs at the Colisée in Roubaix and has gained new creative impetus with the appointment of American choreographer Carolyn Carlson as artistic director. Its rehearsal studios are in a former textile factory that is also home to the dance company **Dans la Rue de Danse**. Look out for the wide-ranging programme of the annual summer festival **Danse à Lille**, which focuses on young choreographers from all over the world.

The magnificently restored interior of the Opéra de Lille

As well as museums, contemporary art venues include **Espace Le Carré**, in part of the old Halle aux Sucres in the Quartier Royale; the **Maison Folie de Wazemmes** *(see page 50)*; the **Condition Publique** *(see pages 63–4)*; **La Malterie** (<www.lamalterie.com>), a converted brewery; and **Galerie de l'Atelier 2**, in an old farm building in Villeneuve d'Ascq.

Cinema-going remains a passion in France. The focus for general releases is the rue de Béthune, where the Majestic and the UGC cinemas offer 20 screens between them; many films are screened in VO (original language with French subtitles). Venues for repertory arts cinema programming and themed festivals are **L'Univers** (16 rue Danton), **Le Meliés** in Villeneuve d'Ascq, and **Le Fresnoy** Studio National des Arts Contemporain in Tourcoing.

MUSIC AND NIGHTLIFE

Lille's main music venue is the **Aéronef** (<www.aeronef-spectacles.com>), which moved in the 1990s to Euralille. Its programme ranges from rock bands to techno DJs. Another long-established venue is the **Cave aux Poètes** (<www.cave auxpoetes.com>) in Roubaix. Big-name rock groups and *variété* singers often play at the 5,000-capacity **Le Zénith** (part of the Grand Palais complex). More local bands and rising talents of all genres play at **Le Biplan** (<www.lebiplan.org>) in Wazemmes, **Le Splendid** in Lille-Fives, **Le Grand Mix** (<www.le

La Vie est un Long Fleuve Tranquille

Life is indeed a long, tranquil river for the wealthy bourgeois Monsieur and Madame Le Quesnoy and their large brood of children, that is, until they discover that the local midwife had swapped one of their children at birth with a baby from the other side of the tracks (or in this case, the canal) and they decide to take back the missing Momo from the Groseilles, a family of petty criminals and scroungers, who live on a housing estate. Etienne Chatilliez's comic film made in 1988 has become a cult piece of French cinema.

The director, who was born in Roubaix in 1952, filmed in several parts of the Lille conurbation: the exterior of the Le Quesnoys' grand *belle époque* patrician's house can be seen at 118 rue Jean Jaurès in Villeneuve d'Ascq; other scenes take place around the canal, as Momo (brilliantly played by a young Benoît Magimel) initiates his new siblings into the delights of illicit bathing in the Deûle. Chatilliez gleefully injects gently malicious humour into class differences, hypocrisy and social mores. There are plenty of clichés but also, ultimately, humanity, tenderness and, even, optimism, as Momo flits between the two families and suggests that the generational gap is bigger than the class one.

grandmix.com>) in Tourcoing, **La Malterie** *(see page 87)*, **Maison Folie des Trois Moulins** and **La Condition Publique** *(see page 63)*.

Drummers at the Braderie

Jazz fans should check out the first-rate line-up for the annual **Planètes Jazz** festival in Tourcoing. More pub-rock and student type bands can be found in the cluster of bars along rue de Masséna and rue de Solférino.

Late-night bars in Lille really are late – most stay open until around 3am, while clubs open until 5am or later. As well as traditional cocktail venues, such as the **Tudor Inn** (12 rue de la Vieille Comédie) just off place Rihour and the **Bateau Ivre** (41 rue Lepelletier), or friendly *bobo* (bourgeois bohemian) hangout **L'Autrement Dit** (14 rue Royale), a wave of sleek, late-night designer bars has hit Lille in the past couple of years, some of which put on lounge music or showcase easy-listening DJs, such as sophisticated bar-restaurant **Ghosn** (14 rue Massena) and **L'Absolu** (48 bis rue de l'Hôpital Militaire; <www.l-absolu.com>). **Le Kremlin Café** (51 rue Jean-Jacques Rousseau), as the name suggests, is a Russian-themed bar with red walls, bust of Lenin and a long list of flavoured vodkas and vodka cocktails. Upmarket, all-night **Le Sybaris** (79 rue d'Angleterre) has a choice of rooms, varied styles of music and a huge list of cocktails and whiskies. The **Network Café** (15 rue du Faisan), with a lounge area and small dance floor, is the long-standing hangout for Lille's beautiful people and better-off students. **Tchouka Club** (80 rue Barthélémy Delespaul, <www.tchoukaclub.com>) draws a gay-mixed clientele with DJs from the local and Belgian house scene.

SHOPPING

Vieux Lille contains the city's best individual shops. Designer names abound on rue de la Grande-Chaussée, rue des Chats-Bossus and rue Lepelletier, including Sonia Rykiel, Kenzo, Hermès and shoes by Accessoire, bags at Furla, Longchamp and Terre de Bruyère and the upmarket silverware and porcelain of Bernardaud and Christofle. Funkier fashions can be found at **Un Peu Plus au Nord** (19 rue du Curé-St-Etienne), or along **rue Basse**, where you'll find Guess, Hugo Boss, the smart-casual look of Agnès b, original feminine dresses at Cotélac, jewellery, clothes and interior design at Bleu Natier's three outlets, and sophisticated children's wear at Histoire d'Enfants. A host of streetwise fashion stores have recently colonised rue de la Clef, including Desert (stocking Isabelle Marant, Vanessa Bruno, Tsumori Chisato), M&F Girbaud Jeans, G-Star and J-C Shop. Trendy casualwear label Diesel is on place Louise de Bettignies, as is Nathalie de Ruyffelaere, for hats (good for weddings) and jewellery. There's a branch of deparment store Printemps on rue Nationale. Euralille Centre Commercial has a Carrefour supermarket and branches of all sorts of other chains; mass-market chains

Markets are always a good insight into local life. The Marché de Wazemmes is a giant mastodon that sprawls over place de la Nouvelle Aventure and surrounding streets on Sunday morning (smaller market on Tuesday and Thursday), with all sorts of food, clothes, flowers and junk for sale and the whiff of hot snacks from a plethora of countries. There is a much smaller but picturesque food market (Wednesday, Friday and Saturday mornings) on place du Concert in Vieux Lille and on place du Sébastopol near the Théâtre Sébastopol (Wednesday and Saturday mornings).

Fashions on rue Basse

also congregate along rue de Béthune, rue de Paris and the Les Tanneurs shopping centre in the central Lille.

Vieux Lille is also a good source of gifts and homeware. Look for designer carpets at **Lessarge**, contemporary furniture at **Jean Maniglier** (89–95 rue de la Monnaie), porcelain and designer kitchen gadgets at **Dîner Chez Soi** (2 rue du Cirque), and original china, lights and furniture at **Une Fée dans le Grenier** (12 rue Masurel). **La Puce à l'Oreille**, on place Louise de Bettignies, has new and old pine furniture, as well as well-chosen tableware, glass, candles and table linens. Furniture outlets and idiosyncratic gifts abound on rue Esquermoise. **Furet du Nord** on the Grand' Place is one of the largest bookshops in Europe and a local institution; it has a big stationery department, CDs and DVDs, all on a complex maze of levels.

Food is another good buy. There's a branch of the celebrated Boulogne-sur-Mer fromager **Philippe Olivier** (3 rue du Curé St-Etienne), and more fine cheeses at **Aux Bons Pâturages** (54

Boulangerie on rue Basse

rue Basse), where the speciality is cheese tarts with maroilles and other powerful northern cheeses, as well as more exotic combinations, such as peach and gorgonzola. Several good food shops congregate around place aux Oignons, including **L'Abbaye des Saveurs**, which has a huge choice of beers, *ginièvre* and regional specialities. *Gaufres fourés* and chocolates are a must at **Méert** on rue Esquermoise *(see page 102)*, as are the ice creams and chocolates at **Yanka** (75 rue Nationale), the ice creams and sorbets at **Dagniaux** (Grand' Place and 105 rue St-André), which include chicory, *speculoos* and beetroot flavours, and the wines, beers and spirits at **Rohart Vinothèque** on rue Faidherbe.

The big event for antiques lovers and collectors is the gigantic **Grande Braderie de Lille** on the first weekend of September *(see box opposite)*, but there is also a smaller version, the **Fête des Berlouffes** at nearby Wattrelos the following weekend, and a regular **flea market** at Wazemmes on Sunday mornings. There are several classy **antiques shops** in Vieux Lille. Try rue Basse, rue Masurel, rue d'Angleterre and rue Royale, where among the regional items you might be able to find fine period furniture, old waffle irons and religious carvings.

Roubaix is known for its discount factory outlets: **Macarthur Glen** (44 mail de Lannoy), which has boutiques lining a pedestrianised street, and **L'Usine** (228 avenue Alfred Motte), in an imposing renovated textile factory. Both sell previous season's fashions at 30–60 percent discounts. Fashion, casual and sports wear are the main items, although there are also outlets in household linen, furnishing fabrics and kitchen wares. For something more alternative, **La Ressourcerie** (9 rue St-Hubert) gives new life to old furniture and household objects, restoring, recycling or converting items for a new use.

Grande Braderie

Every September, Lille is the setting for the jumble sale to end all jumble sales. The Braderie opens at noon on the first Saturday in September and continues all night and the next day until midnight on Sunday. Stalls extend over some 200km (125 miles) of pavement, drawing around two million visitors a year, not just from northern France, but also Britain, Belgium and the Netherlands.

The Grande Braderie has its origins in the great merchant fair held every year in the Middle Ages – a *franche foire* visited by merchants from all over Europe who were granted safety of passage over the period. It was also the one time of year when valets were permitted to clear out the attics of their lords and sell off the goods. The tradition continues today, and as well as antiques dealers who arrive from all over France to set up stalls on the prized pitches – especially the broad esplanade of boulevard Jean-Baptiste Lebas and around the Porte de Paris – many locals clear out junk from their attics or cellars, laying out blankets on the pavement to sell off old paperbacks and comics, children's toys and pairs of skis. From furniture and chandeliers to all sorts of knick-knacks and ornaments, clothes and advertising memorabilia, there is something for everyone. An essential part of the rite is the consumption of colossal amounts of beer and mussels. Vast mounds of mussel shells pile up outside bars and cafés, and there's a prize for the biggest heap.

SPORTS AND OUTDOOR ACTIVITIES

Spectator Sports

Lille has a premier division **football** team, which is temporarily playing at Villeneuve d'Ascq, while a new stadium is constructed. The Hippodrome de Marcq-en-Barœul (tel: 03 20 89 69 00) is one of France's most active **racetracks**, used for trotting races *(le trot attelé)* and flat racing *(le galop)*, including night-time floodlit race meetings. There is also a major annual international **athletics** meeting held at Villeneuve d'Ascq every June.

Running the half marathon during the Lille Braderie

Sporting Activities

Somewhere within Lille Métropole you'll be able to practise pretty much every sport you can think of from golf (eight courses), tennis and horse-riding to go-karting and *escalade* (climbing). There is even a dry ski slope on a reclaimed slag heap at Loisinord at Noeux-les-Mines, southwest of Lille near the A26 motorway.

Cycling is a very popular activity in the north of France, as it is in neighbouring Belgium, and bicycles can be hired next to Gare Lille Flandres. If you're an experienced rollerblader, join in the popular Friday night **roller rally** (tel: 06 79

07 74 43; <www.rol.asso.fr>) around the streets of Lille; a gentler version is available to families on alternate Sunday afternoons. There is an Olympic-size public **swimming pool** on avenue Marx Dormoy, near the Deûle.

Sometimes dubbed 'the hell of the north', the region's most famous sporting event is the annual Paris–Roubaix cycle race, founded over a century ago and notorious for its arduous over-the-cobbles section. The 260-km (160-mile) race, held on the second Sunday of April, begins in Compiègne, north of Paris, and finishes at the Vélodrome de Roubaix.

If you need to work out in a **gym**, some of the more upmarket hotels have fitness centres. Inside the Centre Commercial Euralille, there's a large, modern branch of the Moving fitness chain, which has lots of fitness apparatus, weights and a large variety of classes; day membership is available.

In the area, the Monts de Flandres are popular for **walking** and **cycling** at weekends, while nearer to the centre are the Parc du Héron in Villeneuve d'Ascq and Parc de Septentrion at Marcq-en-Barœul. **Sailing** and other **watersports** can be practised at the Prés du Hem at Armentières (tel: 03 20 44 04 60).

LILLE WITH CHILDREN

Lille is an easy city to manage with children. The old centre, Vieux Lille, is compact and easy to walk around. For the more far-flung attractions, the driverless VAL **Métro** is fun in itself, especially if you avoid rush hours and sit at the front, which gives a distinctly roller-coaster sensation as you wind round the tunnels. The free **zoo** in the Bois de Boulogne is small in scale and very popular with Lillois families at weekends. It's possible to see many of the animals from fairly close up. Nearby, **boat trips** around the port leave from the Pont de la Citadelle, and there's a marionette **puppet the-**

atre in the Jardin Vauban. The underwater world is on brilliant display at **Nausicaa** *(see page 77)*, in Boulogne-sur-Mer. Many museums and theatres put on activities for children, especially on Wednesday (when there is no school) and in school holidays. The **Grand Bleu theatre** stages productions aimed at a young public, while the **Orchestre du Nord** has a programme of children's concerts. The **Musée d'Histoire Naturelle** *(see page 48)* is an old-fashioned natural history museum. The more modern **Forum des Sciences** *(see page 56)* in Villeneuve d'Ascq includes a special section for three- to six-year-olds. As well as its great setting, **La Piscine** *(see page 60)* in Roubaix has a tactile section, where children can learn about textiles by touching fabrics in different boxes. If splashing about is more their scene, La Piscine's replacement nearby is a fun pool.

Eating out with children is a normal part of French life. Mussels and chips at **Aux Moules** *(see page 136)* and a tea-time treat in the tea room at **Méert** *(see page 102)* are classic choices, as is brunch at the **Basilic Café** *(see page 136)* after the Sunday-morning market on place du Concert (less crowded than Wazemmes' market). Café standards including quiche (or local variant, the cheesy tarte aux maroilles), omelettes and mussels are often popular with kids. Many restaurants have children's menus, often along burger-and-chips lines, or will prepare a suitable dish. For something more imaginative, many restaurants will produce an extra plate to share with a small child, or allow a child to eat only a starter.

Exotic fish at Nausicaa

Calendar of Events

1 January *Nouvel An* New Year's Day (public holiday).
6 January *Fête des Rois* Epiphany.
February or March *Carnaval de Dunkerque* Processions and herring-throwing mark the start of Lent.
March *Festival du Film Court de Lille* Short film festival; *Repérages* Dance festival featuring young international choreographers.
April *Paris–Roubaix* Historic cycling race.
April or May *Journées Régionales des Villes Fortifiées* A chance to visit Vauban's fortified citadels, at Lille, Bergues and Gravelines.
May *International Soup Festival; Scènes Etrangères* International dance and theatre festival (first two weeks in May); *Les Transphotographiques* Photo exhibitions by leading international photographers, shows by local artists (mid-May to mid-June); *Franche Foire de Tourcoing* Medieval festivities include minstrels, jesters, bear-tamers, jousting and lots of dressing up; *Wazemmes Accordion* Big celebrations with accordion music in the Wazemmes district (end of May).
June *Latitudes Contemporaines* Contemporary dance festival.
14 July *Le Quatorze Juillet* Bastille Day (public holiday) commemorates the 1789 Revolution.
July–August *Festival Lille Clef de Soleil* Classical music performed in churches and museums.
September *Braderie de Lille* Colossal jumble sale and antiques fair on the streets of Lille (first weekend in September; *see page 93*); *Journées du Patrimoine* Architectural heritage weekend (third weekend in September).
November *Planètes Jazz Festival Tourcoing* French and international jazz talents; *Question de Genre* Gay and lesbian film festival. *Transculturelles* Multicultural, multidisciplinary arts festival in Roubaix.
December *Fête de St-Nicolas* (6 Dec) The traditional start of Christmas: St Nicholas arrives on his donkey to distribute sweets to children; *Braderie de l'Art de Roubaix* Over 24 hours, artists and designers recycle objects into art; *Marché de Noël* Christmas market on place Rihour and a Ferris wheel on the Grand' Place. *Au Rayon Burlesque* Clowns and clowning.

EATING OUT

Beer, *houblon* (hops), *chicorée* and chicory, *ginièvre* (juniper gin), *speculoos* (brown sugar spice biscuits) and sugar all perfume the cuisine of northern France, which, as with other aspects of Lillois culture, has developed over the centuries into a unique Franco-Flemish mix. As with everywhere in France, eating out is an important part of daily life, and there are restaurants to suit all moods and budgets, from grand establishments to simple bistros and brasseries, many of which proudly retain regional traditions and local ingredients. But that is not to say that northern cooking is standing still: several of the city's best restaurants have joined together in the Club des Tables Gourmandes to promote the region's often unduly underrated cuisine. And many creative chefs use regional ingredients to

Café society on Lille's Grand' Place

invent new flavours or put a new twist on forgotten dishes, inspired by market produce, from beef with rhubarb to beetroot ice cream.

For centuries, carts pulled by sturdy Boulonnaise dray horses brought fish from the Channel ports to the French capital in less than 24 hours, thus ensuring the fish's freshness. In 1848 the arrival of steam trains put an end to this race against time, but since 1991, the Route de Poisson has been revived, every two years, on the last weekend of September, when horse-drawn carts once again follow the old cart tracks from Boulogne and try to reach Paris in less than 24 hours.

Regional Dishes

Arguably the best-known regional speciality is the impossible-to-pronounce *potjevleesch*, a sort of layered terrine of assorted white meats (pork, veal, rabbit, chicken) with carrots and onions in jelly, which is generally served as a starter, accompanied by a small salad. Other popular starters are *tarte aux maroilles* or *flamiche aux maroilles* (a powerful cheese and cream open tart) and *tarte aux poireaux* (leek tart), usually served warm. *Langue Lucullus*, smoked ox tongue studded with foie gras, is a speciality of Valenciennes.

Beer features widely in sauces used in dishes such as *coq à la bière*, *turbot à la bière* and delicious warming *carbonnade de boeuf.* In fact, this dish of pieces of beef slow-cooked in beer with caramelised onions and crumbled *pain d'épices* (spice bread) is one of several sweet-savoury combinations loved in the region. Others include *tarte à la vergeoise*, a brown sugar-and-chicory tart, and *lapin aux pruneaux*, rabbit stewed with prunes, supposedly introduced by Polish miners. The *hochepot* or hotpot is a traditional mixed meat-and-vegetable stew, while pungent maroilles and Vieux Lille cheeses are often made into powerful sauces to accompany steaks or other cuts of meat.

The fish is also excellent here, thanks to the proximity of the ports at Dunkerque and Boulogne-sur-Mer. Superb turbot, John Dory, sole and coquilles St-Jacques again all might appear in beer sauces, while *waterzoï* is a refined soup-like creamy stew made with assorted white fish poached with a julienne of leeks and other vegetables (it can also be made with chicken instead of fish). Another delicacy is *crevettes grises*, tiny North Sea shrimps, which make a great starter or appetiser, crunched whole (except the head, you don't need to shell them); they also appear in various fritters and sauces.

As for *moules frites* (mussels and chips)… Well, they are served all year round at most brasseries (and are the speciality at pretty 1930s' Aux Moules, *see page 136*), but the one time they are absolutely compulsory is during the Grande

The Belgian influence is seen in *moules frites*

Gorgeous goat's cheese salad

Braderie when you will find them everywhere, and the café with the highest pile of mussel shells wins a prize.

Chicory, cauliflowers and leeks may be braised or made into gratins, chicory and beetroot are also served as salads, while red cabbage is cooked with spices and served with meat. Potatoes grown in the area include the tiny, elongated *ratte de Touquet*, which has a delicate nutty flavour that makes it a favourite in salads, steamed, or tossed in butter.

For dessert, you'll find all sorts of tarts and French favourites, such as chocolate mousse, but also those ever-present local flavourings of *chicorée* (made from the dried root of a plant similar to chicory), sugar, *speculoos* (brown sugar spice biscuits), *ginièvre* (juniper gin) and hops, in desserts such as simple *tarte au sucre* – a sweet short pastry glazed with egg and caramelised brown sugar topping – rhubarb tart or *chicorée*-flavoured crème brulée.

Gaufres fourés, thin, slightly crispy waffles handmade in a tiny mould and filled with sweet vanilla cream, were the favourite cake of Lille-born Charles de Gaulle, and are still a treat at tea room Méert, where they have been made since 1761. *Gaufres fourés* flavoured with vanilla, *chicorée*, rum or *ginièvre* are also made at the Boulangerie Brigant in Houplines.

Cheeses

Regional cheeses are mostly strong and pungent. Maroilles is a square, semi-soft cheese first made by monks in the 10th century and still produced in the Thierarche and Avesnois areas. The orangey-red rind is sometimes washed in beer. Vieux Lille is a variety of maroilles, ripened in Lille with a grey rind, while fresh, young maroilles is sometimes made into a dolphin-shaped Dauphin rolled in spices and herbs. Much milder are a mimolette, a deep-orange, Gouda-like cheese that is sometimes matured until it is brick hard and dry, and the mild Mont des Cats, which is made in a monastery and tastes similar to St-Paulin.

Time for Tea

If you've got a sweet tooth or just want a calm afternoon pause, then Lille has some scenic tea rooms.

Méert *27 rue Esquermoise, tel: 03 20 57 07 44.* Founded in 1761, this pâtissier and chocolatier is a Lille institution. The beautiful galleried interior with its tiers of shelves dates from 1839; there's also a colourful, chandelier-lit tea room behind. The *gaufres fourés* are a cult item, but the bitter chocolate tart is phenomenal.

Paul *8–12 rue de Paris, tel: 03 20 44 72 56.* Paul now has hundreds of branches across France and even in London, but the original bakery was founded in Lille in 1889. This branch in an ornate Flemish building has a pretty restaurant, serving afternoon teas and more formal meals.

La Maison du Moulin d'Or *31 place du Théâtre, tel: 03 20 55 00 10.* The Moulin d'Or in the Rang de Beauregard was for generations a much-loved purveyor of ladies' underwear and it still proclaims corsetry along the façade. Now the owner's son has turned it into an elegant café, keeping much of the original interior and the grand staircase in the centre. Already nicknamed 'the underwear café' by some, it has become a new intellectual hangout and a great place to pause in the afternoon.

Tous les Jours Dimanche *13 rue Masurel, tel: 03 28 36 05 92.* Settle into one of the decrepit sofas or old cinema seats at this relaxed tea room-cum-*brocante* near the cathedral. As well as a wide choice of teas and homemade cakes, it also serves light lunches.

Estaminets and Brasseries

Cakes from Pâtisserie Méert

A convivial atmosphere and lovingly maintained traditions are almost as essential as the food in the *estaminet*, the specifically northern French type of café, where you can often play old-fashioned games or listen to traditional music, as well as eating and drinking regional specialities. At one time a dying institution, the *estaminet* has returned to fashion in both rural Flanders and Lille, where some of the more authentic *estaminets* such as T'Rijsel (the old Flemish name for Lille) and Chez La Vieille in rue de Gand, with their brick walls, wooden tables, bric-à-brac and old photographs, have been created only in the past few years.

Brasseries are another typical eating place. The classic repertoire includes mussels, steaks and grilled fish, along with regional dishes. Often large and busy, they range from the hectic open-all-hours establishments around the railway station to beautiful *belle époque* and art deco institutions, such as Alcide, Chez André and Aux Moules.

Beer and Ginièvre

Beer is taken seriously here – at one time there were hundreds of small breweries in the city – and over the past few years there has been a revival in artisanal production. The

Beer and a little *ginièvre*

biggest brewery in the area is Jenlain near Valenciennes, but Lille also has its own microbrewery, Les Trois Brasseurs, just in front of the Gare Lille Flandres; since the 1980s it has made unfiltered, unpasteurised beers on the premises. Varieties of beer include *blonde* (lager), *brune* (bitter with a high proportion of hops), *ambrée* (russet-coloured beer), the rare Blanche de Lille, a pearly-coloured wheat beer, made with pale malts and brewed in the area since the 13th century, and special seasonal beers, such as the *bière de Noël*, a dark, high-alcohol beer produced at Christmas, and *bière de mars*, the first brew of the year.

Ginièvre, or juniper gin, was the staple drink of textile workers and miners in the 19th and early 20th centuries. Today production is only a fraction of what it used to be, but artisanally produced *ginièvre* is making a comeback as an apéritif (served neat and chilled), to accompany smoked fish, or as an ingredient in sauces and sorbets. Although the name is similar to gin, only juniper is used to flavour the alcohol, rather than the blend of herbs in English gin; the flavour is closer to whisky. The traditional spirit is a fiery, throat-rasping blend of 80 percent rye and 20 percent malt, but the Distillerie de Wambrechies *(see page 70)* has also recently developed a smoother pure malt variety that can be aged like whisky.

To Help You Order...

Do you have a table?	**Avez-vous une table?**
The bill, please	**L'addition s'il vous plaît**
I would like (a/an/some)...	**Je voudrais (du/de la/des)...**

...and Read the Menu

ail	garlic
agneau	lamb
asperges	asparagus
bar	sea bass
bœuf	beef
cabillaud	cod
caille	quail
canard	duck
cerises	cherries
champignons	mushrooms
chou	cabbage
choufleur	cauliflower
daurade	sea bream
dinde	turkey
échalotes	shallots
endive	chicory
épinards	spinach
farci	stuffed
flamiche	savoury tart
foie	liver
fraises	strawberries
framboises	raspberries
fromage	cheese
glace	ice cream
haricots verts	green beans
homard	lobster
huîtres	oysters
jambon	ham
moules	mussels
œufs	eggs
oignons	onions
pâtes	pasta
petits pois	peas
pintade	guinea fowl
poire	pear
poireaux	leeks
pomme	apple
pomme de terre	potato
porc	pork
potjevleesch	layered white-meat terrine
poulet	chicken
prune	plum
pruneau	prune
raisins	grapes
riz	rice
rognon	kidney
rouget	red mullet
saucisse	sausage
saumon	salmon
thon	tuna
truite	trout
veau	veal
volaille	poultry

HANDY TRAVEL TIPS

An A–Z Summary of Practical Information

A

ACCOMMODATION (see also RECOMMENDED HOTELS, page 130)

Hotels. Central Lille has around 50 hotels offering some 3,000 rooms, ranging from four-star luxury (the Hermitage Gantois) to no-star establishments, though the majority are two- or three-star. Ratings are based on factors such as size of room and reception services, not necessarily on cleanliness or welcome. Prices for a double room are for two people, but many hotels also have suites or some triple or quadruple rooms, or can add a cot (*lit bébé*) or folding bed (*lit pliant* or *lit d'appoint*) for a child.

Alongside small, privately run hotels, several of the hotels in Lille belong to big groups, notably Accor, which owns the Sofitel and Mercure (upmarket), Novotel and Ibis (medium-range), Etap and Formule 1 (budget) chains. Within Lille itself, the majority of hotels do not have restaurants, though they do serve breakfast and may also have a bar. In smaller towns and rural areas, the majority of hotels also have restaurants. Outside Lille, with a few upmarket château hotel exceptions or the modern budget chains around city edges and motorways, the majority of hotels are simple family-run affairs. In small towns and rural areas, those affiliated to the independent organisation Logis de France are often reliable. Hotels can be quite scarce in rural areas, but there are a growing number of *chambres d'hôtes* (B&Bs).

Bon Week-end en Villes is a scheme that offers two nights for the price of one (either Friday and Saturday or Saturday and Sunday) at weekends at participating hotels. You must state that you want this tariff when booking.

Aparthotels/*Résidences Hôtelières*. As the name implies, an aparthotel, such as those belonging to the Citadines group, is a cross between a hotel and an apartment. It generally consists of a studio or one-bedroom flat with an equipped kitchenette. Aparthotels have reception facilities, and often offer breakfast if desired, but a lesser degree of service than in a hotel. They can be a good option when travelling with children, if you don't want to eat in restaurants all the time. Look for discounts for longer stays.

Do you have a single/ double room?	**Avez-vous une chambre simple/double?**
I would like to reserve a room with double bed/ twin beds and bath/shower.	**Je voudrais réserver une chambre avec grand lit/ deux lits et bain/douche.**
Is the hotel air conditioned?	**Est-ce que l'hôtel est climatisé?**
Is breakfast included?	**Est-ce que le petit déjeuner est compris?**

Chambres d'Hôtes. The French equivalent of bed-and-breakfast is growing rapidly in popularity in France and is often an upmarket option, though there are also some very simple places. Many offer beautifully decorated rooms in rural farmhouses, country manors or even châteaux, and there are also some rooms within Lille itself. Under French regulations, *chambres d'hôtes* cannot have more than six bedrooms. Unlike at hotels, breakfast is usually included in the price, while, for an extra fee, some also offer a *table d'hôtes* evening meal, which is usually eaten by all the guests together. Lists are available from tourist offices and from two French organisations, Gîtes de France and Clévacances *(see below)*.

Gîtes or Holiday Rentals. Gîtes are holiday rental properties in rural locations. They range in type from small flats in the buildings of a farm to large country houses with swimming pools. Gîtes de France, <www.gites-de-france-nord.com>, the best-known umbrella organisation, grades properties from one to four ears of corn; Clévacances, <www.clevacances.com>, is a more recently created organisation, with rural holiday lets and holiday apartments in towns.

Youth Hostels. Lille has a YHA-affiliated *auberge de Jeunesse* (youth hostel) at 12 rue Malpart, tel: 03 20 57 08 94, <www.fuaj. org>, not far from the Hôtel de Ville. Central booking, tel: 01 44 89 87 27.

AIRPORTS (see also GETTING THERE)

Lille airport, located 8km (5 miles) southeast of the centre at Lesquin (tel: 08 91 67 32 10, <www.lille.aeroport.fr>), is served mainly by internal flights, with some flights from other European cities; there is a shuttle connection to Lille Europe station. The principal international airports are Paris Charles de Gaulle (<www.aeroportsdeparis.fr>), which is served by frequent direct high-speed trains (approximately 50 minutes) to Lille, and Brussels Zaventum (<www.brusselsairport.be>), about 38 minutes by train to Lille.

B

BICYCLE HIRE

Bicycles can be hired from Ch'ti Vélo (10 avenue Willy Brandt; tel: 03 28 53 07 49; <http://chti-velo.fr>), next to Gare Lille Flandres. Price from €1/hr, €3/half day, €5 full day.

BUDGETING FOR YOUR TRIP (see also PUBLIC TRANSPORT)

In one of the poorer regions of France, Lille is a relatively inexpensive city, although it is more expensive than the surrounding area and you can easily splurge on a good restaurant if you so desire.

Hotels. The main expense is likely to be accommodation, although hotels in France generally give good value for money compared to those in other locations in Western Europe. In central Lille, expect to spend about €60 for two per night in a budget hotel, €80–120 in a mid-range hotel and around €150–200 in the top-category hotels. Breakfast (generally not included in the price) costs from around €6 or €7 in a budget hotel and perhaps as much as €17 in a luxury one.

Food. Lille has restaurants and brasseries to suit all budgets, as well as a wide variety of snack stands. Expect to pay from around €15 for three courses, not including wine, in a budget restaurant, between €20 and €30 in a good bistro and €50 or more in a haute-cuisine one. Many places also offer good-value lunch menus. At a café or bar expect to pay €1.50–2 for a coffee, €2–3 for *un demi* (25cl) of lager – prices may be slightly lower standing at the bar and slightly more if you sit outside on the terrace. A sandwich will cost around €3.50.

Sightseeing. Most museums and monuments charge an admission fee – generally between €3 and €6; there may be an extra charge for special exhibitions. For guided tours expect to pay between €5 and €8. If you are planning a fair amount of museum visiting, the Lille City Pass is a good deal *(see below)*.

Entertainment. Cinema tickets cost €6–8, tickets at the opera range from €5 to €60, and theatre tickets are around €20.

City Pass. If you are planning intensive sightseeing, then the Lille Métropole City Pass (Pass Libre Accès), available from the tourist office, can be a good deal. Available for one (€15), two (€30) or three (€45) days, it gives free access to numerous museums and monuments, selected guided tours, unlimited use of public transport and reduced admission prices on entertainment. The three-day version also covers additional sights in the region and TER regional trains.

C

CAR HIRE (See also DRIVING)

Numerous international and local car-hire firms have offices in Gare Lille Europe and around Gare Lille Flandres. These include: **Avis** , tel: 03 20 06 35 55, <www.avis.fr>; **Budget**, tel: 03 28 36 55 66, <www.budget.com>; **Hertz**, tel: 03 28 36 28 70, <www.hertz.fr>; and

Rentacar, tel: 03 20 40 20 20, <www.rentacar.fr>. To hire a car the driver must have a valid driving licence and be over 21. A car is useful if you want to explore the region or further parts of the Métropole, but within Lille itself, it is often easier to walk or use public transport.

I'd like to rent a car	**Je voudrais louer une voiture**
now/tomorrow	**tout de suite/demain**
for one day/a week	**pour une journée/une semaine**

CHILDREN

Most hotels will happily add a cot (*lit bébé*) or folding bed (*lit pliant, lit d'appoint*) for a child in the parents' room, if there is space; some charge a small amount, while others offer it for free for youngsters under a certain age (usually 12). Children are generally welcome in restaurants, and if there is no special menu, restaurants will often suggest a dish or allow a child to share with a parent or order only part of a menu. Children get in free at many museums and galleries, but the age limit varies. Museums that do charge will have a *tarif réduit* (reduced entry fee) for children.

CLIMATE

Lille has a temperate climate, much like that of England's Kent on the other side of the Channel. Winters are relatively mild but can be damp and foggy; summers are warm. It can rain in any season. When driving in the countryside, beware of early-morning fog and also winds that whip over the flat land. For weather forecasts tel: 08 92 68 02 59 or look at <www.meteofrance.fr>.

CLOTHING

Light clothes are suitable in summer, but you may want a jacket or cardigan in the evening. Bring warm clothes and a coat in winter and an umbrella at any time of year. The French generally dress fairly casually, but will dress up where appropriate – don't wear shorts if you're going to a smart restaurant.

CRIME AND SAFETY

Lille is a relatively safe place, but like any large city, certain precautions apply. Don't walk across parks alone late at night and be careful of pickpockets around the railway stations. If you are robbed, you should report it at the Commissariat de Police *(see page 122)*.

CUSTOMS AND ENTRY REQUIREMENTS

EU citizens need only a passport or identity card. You should carry a passport/ID with you at all times. Visitors from Australia, Canada, New Zealand and the US also do not need a visa for stays of up to three months. Citizens of other countries should enquire at the French embassy or consulate before leaving home.

As France is part of the Schengen agreement, passports are generally not checked between France and Belgium (though they are checked between France and the UK). But, as possession of drugs is illegal in France, cars and coaches arriving from Belgium are sometimes stopped if they are believed to have come from Amsterdam.

In theory there are no customs limits within the EU for alcohol or tobacco, providing it is for personal requirements, which is generally calculated as a maximum of 10 litres of spirits, 20 litres of fortified wine, 90 litres of wine, 110 litres of beer, 200 cigars or 3,200 cigarettes. From outside the EU, the limits are 200 cigarettes, 1 litre of spirits and 2 litres of wine.

D

DISABLED TRAVELLERS

By law, newly built hotels and restaurants have to have wheelchair access, with specially adapted doorways and lavatories, but access is often more difficult in historic buildings, so ring ahead to check. The-

brochures *Lille Accommodation* and *Lille: Restaurants & Night-Life* indicate establishments with wheelchair access or adapted rooms. Many museums are wheelchair accessible at least in part, and some also organise special visits for blind or partially sighted visitors. Lille Métro system is accessible for wheelchairs, with lifts at all stations.

DRIVING

Drive on the right. British, US, Canadian and Australian driving licences are valid. You should also have your insurance and car registration documents with you. Within urban areas, the speed limit is generally 50km/h (30mph), with 30km/h (19mph) in some residential zones. Outside the city, roads are divided into *autoroutes* (A), *routes nationales* (N), *routes départementales* (D) and tiny rural *routes communales* (C). On autoroutes the speed limit is 130km/h (81mph), except where indicated. On N and D roads, except within built-up areas, the speed limit is generally 90km/h (56mph), with 110km/h (68mph) on dual carriageways. Note that speed limits are increasingly strictly enforced, and there are now automatic radar machines (as well as gendarmes in cars) on many *autoroutes* and *routes nationales*.

Parking. Parking can be difficult in the centre of Lille. The best idea is to use the public car parks under the Grand' Place and place de la République, and by the railway stations, or the large car parks by the ring road at the Grand Palais and Champs de Mars, near the Citadelle. The Citadine shuttle bus connects the car parks at the Champ de Mars, Norexpo (Grand Palais) and Porte de Valenciennes, via boulevard de la Liberté through central Lille.

driving licence	**permis de conduire**
car registration papers	**carte grise**
Fill the tank, please.	**Le plein, s'il vous plaît.**
My car has broken down.	**Ma voiture est en panne.**
There's been an accident.	**Il y a eu un accident.**

Road Signs. Most signs are the standard pictographs used throughout Europe, but you may encounter the written signs below as well:

Déviation	Diversion (detour)
Péage	Toll
Priorité à droite	Yield to traffic from the right
Ralentir	Slow down
Rappel	Restriction continues
Sens interdit	No entry
Sens unique	One way
Serrez à droite/à gauche	Keep right/left
Vous n'avez pas la priorité	Give way

E

ELECTRICITY

Electricity in France runs on 220 volts. UK visitors should bring an adaptor plug for electrical appliances; North American visitors will need a transformer.

EMBASSIES AND CONSULATES

The UK and US both have consulates in Lille, other embassies and consulates are in Paris. Phone for opening hours.
Australia: 4 rue Jean-Rey, 75015 Paris, tel: 01 40 59 33 00.
Canada: 35 avenue Montaigne, 75008 Paris, tel: 01 44 43 29 00.
Ireland: 4 rue Rude, 75116 Paris, tel: 01 44 17 67 00.
New Zealand: 7ter rue Léonard de Vinci, 75116 Paris, tel: 01 45 01 43 43.
South Africa: 59 quai d'Orsay, 75007 Paris, tel: 01 53 59 23 23.
UK: 11 square Dutilleul, 59000 Lille, tel: 03 20 12 82 72; emergency tel: 03 20 54 79 82.
US: 107 rue Royale, 59000 Lille, tel: 03 28 04 25 00.

EMERGENCIES

In case of an emergency, telephone:

- **Ambulance** (SAMU) 15
- **Fire** (Sapeurs-Pompiers) 18
- **Police** 17

From a mobile phone the emergency number is 112

Police!	**Police!**
Fire!	**Au feu!**
Help!	**Au secours!**

G

GAY AND LESBIAN TRAVELLERS

As a large city with a huge student population, Lille is generally gay tolerant, with several gay and gay-friendly bars and clubs, notably on rue Royale, and a Gay Pride week in June. A good source of information is Gaykitschcamp (38 bis rue Royale, tel: 03 20 06 33 91, <www.gaykitschcamp.com>), a gay bookshop and documentation centre, which also organises Question de Genre, a gay film festival each November/December.

GETTING THERE

By Boat. Lille is within easy distance of the Channel ports of Boulogne-sur-Mer (118km/73 miles), Calais (110km/68 miles) and Dunkerque (71km/44 miles). Calais is served by frequent ferries to and from Dover run by SeaFrance (UK tel: 0870 571 1711, <www.seafrance.com>) and P&O-Stena Lines (UK tel: 0870 598 0333, <www.poferries.com>). Norfolk Line (UK tel: 0870 870 1020, France tel: 03 28 59 01 01; <www.norfolkline-ferries.com>) runs between Dover and Dunkerque, and Speedferries (UK tel: 0870 2200 570, France tel: 03 21 10 50 00, <www.speedferries.com>) has introduced a high-speed (50 mins) catamaran service between Dover and Boulogne-sur-Mer.

Eurotunnel. (UK tel: 08705 353535; France tel: 08 10 63 03 04, <www.eurotunnel.com>). The tunnel under the Channel transports cars by train on Le Shuttle between Folkestone and Calais, taking about 35 mins. *(See below for information on the Eurostar.)*

By Train. Lille is served by frequent Eurostar trains, UK tel: 0870 518 6186, <www.eurostar.com> direct from London (approx. 1hr 40 mins), Brussels (approx. 38 mins) and by the French high-speed TGV network from Paris (1hr). There are 24 TGVs a day between Paris and Lille, and direct trains to 70 other French cities, including Bordeaux, Lyon, Marseille, Nice and Toulouse, as well as to Paris Charles de Gaulle airport and Disneyland Resort Paris. There is also a local network of regional trains (TER). For mainline train information, ticket sales and other information tel: 3635 within France, +33 (0)8 92 35 35 35 from outside France, or visit <www.sncf.fr>. *(See also page 125.)*

By Car. Lille is well served by a dense network of motorways, which run directly into a ring road around the city centre. The city is 110km (68 miles) from Calais by the A16 and A25, 220km (137 miles) from Paris by the A1, 123km (76 miles) from Brussels by the A27, 71km (44 miles) from Dunkerque by the A25, 73km (45 miles) from Ghent (Gand) by the A22. If coming from the UK, cars can be transported either by car ferry or by Eurotunnel *(see above)*. Most French motorways are toll roads (*péages*), though not the sections in Lille Métropole. *(See also Car Hire and Driving.)*

GUIDES AND TOURS

Audio Tours. Mobile phone guides available in English offer chatty commentaries on around half a dozen sights in Lille (tel: 08 92 68 25 11 + 008 020) or Roubaix (tel: 08 92 68 25 11 + 010 000), allowing you to walk round the city at your own pace and switch on and off as you wish.

Bus Tours. Lille runs a popular 50-minute City Tour by bus, which leaves every hour from in front of the tourist office (May–Oct daily 10am–6pm, Nov–Apr daily 10am–5pm), with recorded commentary in eight languages including English. The tour passes the main sights and cleverly supplements what you can see with recorded material and photos, paintings and archive documents shown on screens.

Walking Tours. If you've seen the main sights and want to get to know specific facets of the Métropole's history and architecture better, consider a walking tour. Most are in French, but there is a weekly two-hour guided tour in English of Vieux Lille every Saturday at 2.30pm. Pick up the booklet from the tourist office.

Boat Trips. Isnor (tel: 03 21 39 15 15; <www.isnor.fr>) runs one-hour boat trips around the port. These leave from the Ecluse (lock) de la Barre, near the Citadelle at the end of boulevard de la Liberté. The company also does longer trips to Wambrechies, taking in a visit to the distillery there.

Helicopter Tours. See Lille from the sky in a 15-minute flight with Opale Fun (contact Lille tourist office for info). Flights leave from Lesquin Airport at 1.30pm on the first Saturday of the month, May–Oct, weather permitting (€75 per person, €70 per person for a family).

H

HEALTH AND MEDICAL CARE

EU visitors are eligible for emergency medical care within the French health service, but should bring the European Health Insurance Card with them (available from post offices or online at <www.dh.gov.uk>)

to be reimbursed. Note that the percentage of the cost reimbursed varies and may be very little for dental work or for opticians. Non-European visitors should make sure they have health insurance.

French medical care is generally of a high standard. If you need to visit a doctor, your hotel should be able to recommend a *médecin généraliste* (general practitioner) in the vicinity. Alternatively, look in the *Yellow Pages (Pages Jaunes).*

There is a 24-hour casualty *(urgences)* department at Hôpital Roger Salengro, boulevard du Professeur Jules Leclercq (tel: 03 20 44 59 62 (switchboard), 03 20 44 61 40 (casualty), Métro CHR B Calmette, part of a huge hospital complex just south of the ring road. SOS Médecins (tel: 03 20 29 91 91) is a 24-hour doctor service which can give advice by phone or make house calls.

Pharmacies. Lille is abundantly supplied with pharmacies (indicated by a green neon cross), and most staff are well-qualified and helpful. After hours, pharmacies will have a notice posted on the door giving details of the nearest *pharmacie de garde*, which is open late or on a Sunday.

L

LANGUAGE

The language spoken in Lille is, of course, French, though most hotels will have a member of staff who speaks at least some English. Note that French is generally more formal than English, and the terms *madame*, *mademoiselle* and *monsieur* are widely used in ordinary conversation. Unless you are addressing children or people you know well, it is polite to use the more formal *vous* rather than the informal *tu* form for 'you'. Across the border in Belgium, the local language is Flemish (similar to Dutch). Some people, mainly the elderly, still speak the local dialect of *Ch'ti*, which has also enjoyed a trendy recent revival among the young *(see box, page 8)*.

Below are just a few useful basic phrases in French:

Do you speak English?	**Parlez-vous anglais?**
I am English/American.	**Je suis anglais(e)/américain(e).**
How much is it?	**C'est combien?**
I don't understand	**Je ne comprends pas.**

LOST PROPERTY

If you leave anything on a train, go in person to the SNCF station, where you will be asked to fill in a form. Property lost elsewhere should be reported to the police at the Commissariat Central, tel: 03 20 50 55 99 *(see Police, page 122)*.

M

MAPS

A free fold-out street map of Lille is available from the tourist office or hotels. There is also a Transpole map of public transport available at Transpole kiosks. If you are planning to explore further afield, it's a good idea to have a Michelin or other similar 1:200,000 road atlas of France or a regional sheet map published by IGN or Michelin.

MEDIA

Newspapers. As well as national dailies *Le Monde*, *Libération* and *Le Figaro*, and sports daily *L'Equipe*, there is also a widely read regional paper *Le Voix du Nord*. *20 Minutes* is one of a growing number of free newspapers combining international news with a local section. *Le Point*, *L'Express* and *Nouvel Observateur* are well-respected weekly news magazines. English dailies and other international newspapers are available on newsstands at Gare Lille Europe and Gare Lille Flandres.

Television. French television includes state channels France 2 and France 3, Arte/le Cinq, commercial channels TF1 and M6, subscription channel Canal+, plus a huge offering available on cable or satellite, such as Canal Jimmy, TMC, 13e Rue and Teva (soap operas and series), LCI (24-hour news), sports, travel and history channels, as well as a variety of foreign chains. In addition, many hotels have CNN or CNBC and BBC World. France 3 has a regional focus. As Lille is close to the border, you will generally also receive Belgian channels, which broadcast many TV series in English with Flemish subtitles.

MONEY

Currency. Since 1 January 2002, the currency in France has been the euro (€), though don't be surprised if you still find the French talking in francs, especially when it comes to large sums of money. A euro is divided into 100 centimes. Cash machines generally issue notes in €10, €20 or €50 denominations; €100, €200 and €500 notes are also issued, but try to avoid the large denomination notes of €200 or €500, which many shopkeepers are unwilling to accept. There are coins for 1, 2, 5, 10, 20 and 50 centimes and 1 and 2 euros.

Exchange Facilities. Note that not all banks have exchange facilities; look for those with a Change sign, including Crédit du Nord (28 place Rihour), open Mon–Fri. There is a Thomas Cook bureau de change at Gare Lille Flandres (place des Buisses), open daily.

I want to change some pounds/dollars.	**Je voudrais changer des livres sterling/dollars.**

ATMs. Cash machines are widespread and can be found outside banks and post offices (and sometimes also mainline railway stations). They operate on global credit and debit systems including Cirrus and Maestro, and are often the simplest way of taking out money.

Credit Cards. Credit cards, especially Visa (often called here by its French name, Carte Bleue), are widely accepted in shops, hotels and restaurants. French-issued cards have a microchip *(puce)* that is read by a machine and validated with the PIN number rather than signing a slip of paper; for any foreign-issued cards with a magnetic band, you will be issued with a slip to sign. There may be a minimum sum required (often around €15). If you lose your credit card or it is stolen, you should telephone the card-issuer to report it *(faire opposition)* on tel: 0892 705 705 (for Visa or MasterCard), tel: 01 47 77 72 00 (for American Express), or tel: 08 10 31 41 59 (for Diners' Club).

Travellers' Cheques. Travellers' cheques are not widely used, but those issued in euros can be cashed at banks.

Do you accept traveller's cheques/this credit card?	**Acceptez-vous les chèques de voyage/cette carte de crédit?**

OPENING HOURS

Banks and Post Offices. Banks generally open Monday to Friday from around 9am to 5pm. Some close at lunchtime, and some are closed on Monday but open on Saturday morning. Post offices generally open Monday to Friday from 8am or 8.30am to 6.30pm and on Saturday morning (from around 8am to noon).

Cafés and Restaurants. Restaurants generally serve food from noon to around 2pm and from 7.30 or 8pm to around 10.30pm. Many restaurants are closed on Monday and Sunday. If you want to eat outside these hours, your best bet is probably a café or brasserie, which often serve food all day and stay open until late. Cafés generally open at around 8am or 9am to serve breakfast. Keep in mind that, as in the rest of France, many restaurants close for all or part of August.

Bars and Clubs. Lille nightlife starts late and goes on late: many bars open from around 6pm until 3am, while clubs tend to start at 10 or 11pm and stay open until 5 or 6am.

Museums. Most museums open from 9 or 10am to 5 or 6pm. Smaller ones sometimes close at lunchtime, and most are closed all day on either Monday or Tuesday.

Pharmacies. Pharmacies (indicated by a green neon cross) generally keep the same hours as shops, and on Sunday will indicate the nearest *pharmacie de garde*.

Shops and Markets. Shops generally open Monday to Saturday, from 9.30am to 7pm. Bakers usually have slightly longer hours. Boutiques in the Euralille shopping centre open 10am–8pm, with the Carrefour supermarket open 9am–10pm. Some shops in the Wazemmes district are open on Sunday morning, and most districts will have a local *épicerie* open until late and on Sunday. Some smaller shops close in August. Lille has a number of local street markets, generally open morning only, two or three days a week *(see also box, page 90)*.

Are you open tomorrow?	**Est-ce que vous ouvrez demain?**

P

POLICE

The main police station is the Commissariat Central de Lille, 5 boulevard Maréchal Vaillant, tel: 03 20 62 47 47.

Where's the nearest police station?	**Où se trouve le commissariat de police le plus proche?**

POST OFFICES

The main post office is at 8 place de la République (corner of boulevard Inkermann and boulevard de la Liberté), but there are several small post offices throughout the city, including ones at 1–3 boulevard Carnot (near the Nouvelle Bourse), 129 rue Colbert (in the Vauban district) and inside the Centre Commercial Euralille. Postage stamps *(timbres)* can also be purchased at tobacconists *(tabacs)*, which is often quicker than queuing at a post office. At the time of writing, a stamp for a standard postcard or letter in France was €0.50, and could be bought in *carnets* (books) of 10, and postage for the rest of Europe was €0.53. Post offices generally also have coin-operated photocopiers and coin-operated machines where you can weigh a letter or parcel and buy the stamps.

PUBLIC HOLIDAYS

There are public holidays on 1 January (Nouvel An), Easter Monday (lundi de Pâcques), 1 May (Fête du Travail), 8 May (end of World War II in Europe), late May (Pentecost Monday), late May/early June (Ascension Thursday), 14 July (le Quatorze Juillet), 15 August (Ascension Day), 1 November (Toussaints), 11 November (Armistice Day) and 25 December (Noël).

Generally banks and public buildings are closed on these days, as are many museums, shops and some restaurants; public transport usually runs to a Sunday timetable. Those holidays most fully observed are 1 January, 1 May, 14 July and 25 December. When a public holiday falls on a Tuesday or Thursday, many French like to take *le pont* (bridge), taking off the intervening day to make a long weekend.

PUBLIC TRANSPORT

Lille Métropole has an extensive network of bus routes, plus two Métro lines and two tramways all linked under the Transpole umbrella. Information is available on Allo Transpole (tel: 08 20 42 40 40) or <www.transpole.fr>. A combined one-day pass costs €3.50, a single journey, allowing changes of transport, costs €1.20 (*carnet* of 10 tickets: €10.20) and a short-hop ZAP ticket (up to three Métro or tram stops, with no changes) costs €0.60. Tickets can be bought at Transpole kiosks at Gare Lille Flandres, Roubaix Eurotéléport and Tourcoing Centre, from bus drivers and from automatic machines at Métro stations and tram stops. *Carnets* and season tickets can also be bought from some tobacconists. Individual tickets should be stamped in the machine before getting on the Métro or on the bus. Day passes should be stamped before their first use. *(See also page 110 for information about the City Pass/ Pass Libre Accès.)*

Buses. You may want to use the bus for some of the more remote parts of Lille Métropole. Most buses run until around 9.30pm, after which there is a more limited Claire de Lune network until 12.30am.

Métro. Lille's high-speed driverless trains, known as the VAL, were the first of their kind and provide fast, efficient transport from central Lille to the edges of the Métropole. At rush hours trains arrive almost every minute, and even early in the morning, in the evening or on a Sunday, the maximum wait should not be more than six minutes. The first trains leave end-of-the-line stations just after 5am Mon–Sat (around 6.30am Sun) and run until around midnight.

Tramway. Two modern tramlines run every 10 to 15 minutes between Lille Gare Flandres and Tourcoing (5.44am–12.23am) and Lille Gare Flandres and Roubaix (5.36am–12.40am).

Mainline Trains. French mainline services are run by the SNCF. Lille is well connected by the TGV *(train de grande vitesse)* high-speed trains to other parts of France *(see page 116)*. A network of regional trains also serves the area, including Arras, Valenciennes, Douai and Calais, and local trains to stations such as Croix, Wasquehal and Tourcoing. The two mainline stations – Lille Flandres (regional trains and TGV services to and from Paris) and Lille Europe (Eurostar and TGV services) – are within easy reach of each other by foot.

Before getting on a train, you must stamp *(composter)* your ticket in the orange machine at the head of the platform – slide it into the slot and the ticket will be stamped and a bite taken out of it. Failure to do so could mean an on-the-spot fine when your ticket is inspected on the train.

Standard ticket rates vary between peak *(période rouge)* and normal *(période bleue)* hours. Various discounts are available on inter-city trips, some of which involve buying a special card, after which discounts of up to 50 percent are offered. Some are available without a card, such as the *Découverte à Deux* for two people travelling together or *Enfant+,* which enables up to five adults travelling with a child under 12 to receive 25 percent off the adult fare.

R

RELIGION

France is a predominantly Roman Catholic country, although only a small percentage of the population attends services. Times of Mass are posted at church entrances. The *Yellow Pages (Pages Jaunes)*, which can be found in most hotel rooms and at all hotel desks, lists places of worship for every faith and denomination.

Lille's synagogue is at 5 rue Auguste Angelier, tel: 03 20 51 12 52. The city's main mosque (Grande Mosquée de Lille) is at 59 rue de Marquillies, tel: 03 20 53 02 65.

S

SMOKING

Smoking is widespread in France, though recent hikes in cigarette taxes mean that the number of smokers has begun to go down. Smoking is now generally banned in theatres, cinemas and on public transport. All TGV carriages are now non-smoking. In theory, restaurants should have a non-smoking section, although in practice non-smoking and smoking sections may be adjacent to one another. Some hotels have non-smoking floors.

T

TAX REFUNDS

Visitors from outside the EU can claim *Detaxe* (a tax refund) on certain purchases made in France, providing they spend over €175 in one day. Ask the shop for a *bordereau de vente à l'exportation.* The tax- refund scheme does not cover food, drink, antiques or works of art.

TAXIS

There are taxi ranks on place des Buisses outside Gare Lille Flandres and on avenue Le Corbusier outside Gare Lille Europe, as well as at various points around town (indicated by a blue-and-white Taxi sign). You can also hail taxis in the street; a taxi is available when the white light on the roof is lit up and unavailable when it is orange. Taxis can also be reserved by phone on tel: 03 20 06 06 06, 03 20 06 64 00 or 03 20 55 20 56.

TELEPHONES

French telephone numbers have 10 figures, which are usually indicated in pairs. Numbers in northeast France begin with 03; mobile phone numbers begin with 06; some new numbers with private telephone operators now start with 07 or 08. Directory enquiries are now available from a number of providers, all starting with 118, including 118000, 118007, 118008, 118218, 118712.

If ringing from abroad dial the international dialling code for France (+33) and leave off the initial '0' from the main number. Telephone boxes generally take phonecards, bought from tobacconists and some supermarkets, but some also take credit cards.

Special-Rate Numbers. Numbers beginning with 0800 are freephone numbers, as are some new four figure numbers beginning with 10; other numbers starting with 08 (and four-figure numbers beginning with 36) have special rates ranging from local rates to premium tariffs.

TIME ZONES

The time in France is one hour ahead of the UK and six hours ahead of the time in New York. Note that the 24-hour clock is widely used in France.

New York	London	**Lille**	Sydney	Auckland
6am	11am	**noon**	8pm	10pm

TIPPING

Service, generally 12.5 percent or 15 percent, is included by law in restaurant bills, but many people leave a small tip, perhaps €2 or €5 in a bistro, more in a smart restaurant if they are happy with the meal and service. It is common practice to leave small change for a drink in a bar or café. In taxi rides, it is appreciated also if you round up to the nearest euro when paying the fare.

Is service included?	**Est-ce que le service est compris?**

TOILETS

There are free toilets in museums and department stores. If using a toilet in a café, it is polite to at least order a coffee at the bar.

Where is the toilet?	**Où sont les toilettes?**

TOURIST INFORMATION

Lille tourist office provides maps and information on sights, entertainment, hotels, restaurants and tours, as well as plenty of leaflets on events and festivals. It also runs a booking service for hotels.

Lille Tourist Office: Palais Rihour, place Rihour, tel: 03 59 57 94 00/ 08 90 39 20 04; <www.lilletourism.com>. Open Mon–Sat 9.30am–6.30pm, Sun 10am–noon and 2–5pm.
Roubaix: 12 place de la Liberté, tel: 03 20 65 31 90, <www.roubaixtourism.net>.
Villeneuve d'Ascq: Château de Flers, chemin Chat Botté, tel: 03 20 43 55 75, <www.villeneuvedascq-tourisme.eu>.
Seclin: 70 rue Roger Bouvry, tel: 03 20 90 12 12, <www.seclin-tourisme.com>.
Tourcoing: 9 rue de Tournai, tel: 03 20 26 89 03, <www.tourcoing-tourisme.com>.
Wambrechies: Mairie, 2 place Général de Gaulle, tel: 03 28 38 84 21.

Information is also available from French Government Tourist Offices outside the country, <www.franceguide.com>. Addresses are as follows:
UK: 178 Piccadilly, London W1V 9AL, tel: 09068 244123.
USA: 444 Madison Avenue, New York NY 10022, tel: 514 288 1904.

Where's the nearest tourist office?	**Où se trouve l'office de tourisme la plus proche?**

W

WEBSITES AND INTERNET ACCESS

<www.cdt-nord.fr>	*Départemental* tourist board site.
<www.lechti.com>	Local events, nightlife and restaurants.
<www.lilletourism.com>	Tourist office site.
<www.lillelanuit.com>	Bars, clubs, nightlife and concerts.
<www.lillemetropole.fr>	Urbanism, culture and sport in the Métropole.
<www.mairie-lille.fr>	Municipal site.
<www.musenor.com>	Museums in the north of France.
<www.transpole.fr>	Local transport information.
<www.vivrealille.com>	Restaurants, bars, culture and sport.
<www.voixdunord.fr>	Regional news.

Internet access

There are WiFi hotspots at many hotels, some cafés and in the Lille Europe and Lille Flandres train stations. One good internet café is Net-K, 13 rue de la Clef, tel: 03 20 55 13 42.

WEIGHTS AND MEASURES

The metric system – a French invention – is universally used.

Y

YOUTH DISCOUNTS AND STUDENT CARDS

Discounts are widely available for students aged under 26, such as reduced-price entry for museums. Because of Lille's large student population, there are often discounts offered on services, such as haircuts, photocopying or sports club membership. You should have a valid ISIC student card. Those aged 12–25 can save up to 25 percent on train travel with the *Découverte* 12–25 tariffs, or up to 50 percent with the *Carte 12/25*.

Recommended Hotels

Lille has a wide range of accommodation, from budget hotels to the luxury Hermitage Gantois. Prices below are for a double room with bath or shower per night, including VAT but not breakfast. An additional tourist tax, which varies according to the hotel's star rating, is charged per person per night. Many business-oriented hotels offer lower rates at weekends. Several hotels participate in the Bon Week-End en Villes scheme (<www.bon-week-end-en-villes.com>), offering two nights for the price of one, starting on a Friday or Saturday. You must book at least 24 hours in advance, mentioning the offer, and confirm by letter, fax or email.

The tourist office offers a central booking service, covering 43 hotels of all standards, in person at the Palais Rihour, by telephone (within France 08 91 56 20 04, from abroad +33 5 59 57 94 00), by fax (03 59 57 94 14) or internet (<www.lilletourism.com>). Accommodation is generally plentiful, but if you want to stay in Lille during the Grande Braderie (first weekend of September), book months ahead.

€€€€	€200 and above
€€€	€120–200
€€	€80–120
€	€80 and under

LILLE

Apart'Hôtel Citadines €€ *83 avenue Willy Brandt, tel: 03 28 36 75 00, fax: 03 20 06 97 82, <www.citadines.com>.* Spacious, light studios and two-room apartments with good kitchens, in the modern Euralille complex overlooking the Tri-Postal and adjoining the Gare Lille Flandres. Apart'hotels are geared towards self-catering, although breakfast is served. Discounts available for longer stays.

Best Western Grand Hôtel Bellevue €€€ *5 rue Jean Roisin, tel: 03 20 57 45 64 , fax: 03 20 40 07 93, <www.grandhotelbellevue.com>.* The glass *porte cochère* entrance (wide enough for a carriage) sets the tone for this old-fashioned hotel, where the young Mozart once stayed. The corridors are a little shabby, but the 60 rooms are spacious and fancifully Louis XV in style. Many overlook dismal courtyards, so ask for one at the rear with a view of the Grand' Place.

Comfort Hôtel Opéra €–€€ *28 rue Anatole France, tel: 03 20 55 25 11, fax: 03 20 06 02 20, <www.hotel-alize-opera.com>.* Rooms in this 1930s' hotel on a side street behind the station are simple, with parquet floors, small beds and nothing in the way of decoration, but there's a pleasant, airy lobby and a jovial, jokey English-speaking manager. The 42 rooms have all been recently renovated.

Crowne Plaza Hôtel €€€–€€€€ *335 boulevard de Leeds, tel: 03 20 42 46 46, fax: 03 20 40 13 14, <www.lille-crowneplaza.com>.* For a taste of Euralille modernity, the copper-covered Crowne Plaza plays a design card, all geometric forms in its light-filled double height lobby and bar. The 121 bedrooms are equally modern, with pale creams, natural wood and Philippe Starck transparent Ghost chairs. There's a restaurant, fitness room and five meeting rooms.

Etap Hôtel Lille Centre € *10 rue de Courtrai, tel: 08 92 68 30 78, fax: 03 28 52 34 15, <www.accorhotels.com>.* If you're looking for seriously cheap, no-frills accommodation then the Etap Hôtel is a convenient, efficient solution, well placed for the old town and the train stations. Rooms all sleep up to three, with a bunk bed posed over the double bed, and have en-suite shower and WC. 92 rooms. Car park.

Hermitage Gantois €€€€ *224 rue de Paris, tel: 03 20 85 30 30, fax: 03 20 42 31 31, <www.hotelhermitagegantois.com>.* Ancient meets hi-tech in this luxurious hotel in a lovely Flemish brick building, which was for centuries a hospice (founded 1462) until converted in 2003. The result is a clever combination of historic features and contemporary touches, from the chapel, wood-panelled salons and courtyard gardens, to the glass-and-steel roof over the reception and bar, flat-screen TVs and smart bathrooms. Restaurant and brasserie.

Hôtel Alliance Couvent des Minimes €€€–€€€€ *17 quai de Wault, tel: 03 20 30 62 62, fax: 03 20 42 94 25, <www.alliance-lille.*

com>. A beautiful rib-vaulted cloister is the centrepiece of this chic hotel in a 17th-century convent, peacefully set by the water's edge near the Citadelle. Spacious, comfortable rooms, most opening on to the gallery above the cloister; those on the third floor are mansarded. A glazed atrium over the courtyard is now a bar and restaurant.

Hôtel Balladins Le Chagnot €€ *24 place de la Gare, tel: 03 20 74 11 87, fax: 03 20 74 08 23, <www.balladins.com>*. This 1950s' hotel above the Trois Brasseurs microbrewery is the best hotel overlooking the Gare Lille Flandres. All rooms have a smart wood-veneered business style, and the breakfast room gives bird's-eye views over the city.

Hôtel Brueghel €€ *5 parvis St-Maurice, tel: 03 20 06 06 69, fax: 03 20 63 25 27, <www. hotel-brueghel.com>*. A creaky vintage lift and cosy hall with yellow walls and purple velvet sofa give a warming welcome at this characterful, good-value hotel near St-Maurice. Rooms, each different, are quite small but spotless; most have been redecorated in pleasant light colours. Higher floors offer views over the rooftops, rue de Paris or the church itself.

Hôtel Carlton €€€–€€€€ *3 rue de Paris, tel: 03 20 13 33 13, fax: 03 20 51 48 17, <www.carltonlille.com>*. In a sweeping, domed corner building, the Carlton is Lille's original 19th-century grand hotel, and even though a steakhouse now occupies part of the ground floor, the hotel still has a certain cachet. Sixty spacious, comfortable bedrooms come with plush period furnishings, air-conditioning and marble bathrooms. There's a fitness room, sauna and a panelled bar. For a splurge, choose the Coupole suite, a circular aerie in the dome itself.

Hôtel Ibis Centre Opéra €€ *21 rue Lepelletier, tel: 03 20 06 21 95, fax: 03 20 74 91 30, <www.ibishotel.com>*. Ibis chain-style functionality at this modern, air-conditioned hotel, and the service is efficient and friendly. Great value for the location in the heart of Vieux Lille.

Hôtel Lille Europe €€ *avenue Le Corbusier, tel: 03 28 36 76 76, fax: 03 28 36 7 77,<www.hotel-lille-europe.com>*. This modern hotel within the Euralille commercial centre is a good budget option with 97 practical rooms and a pleasant glazed breakfast room.

Hôtel Mercure Lille Centre Opéra Le Royal €€€ *2 boulevard Carnot, tel: 03 20 14 71 47, fax: 03 20 14 71 48, <www.mercure.com>*. Renovated and run by the Mercure group, the century-old Le Royal is a hotel with genuine panache. An impressive high-ceilinged hallway with wood panelling, rich fabrics and brass chandeliers leads to a comfortable bar in neo-Flemish style that echoes the Nouvelle Bourse next door. Rooms, decorated in a scheme of burgundy and rich foliate ochre fabric, are very attractive, though on the small side.

Hôtel de la Paix €€ *46 bis rue de Paris, tel: 03 20 54 63 93, fax: 03 20 63 98 97*. The entrance to this 18th-century building is so discreet from the street as to be easy to miss, but the charming interior and the friendly, helpful staff make it a real find. The inside has lots of character, from the leather Chesterfield at the reception to the landing decked out in a striking combination of deep pink and pale green. Rooms are more sober but pleasantly redecorated with wardrobe and mini-bar.

Hôtel des Tours €€€ *27 rue des Tours, tel: 03 59 57 47 00, fax: 03 59 57 47 99, <www.hoteldestours.fr>*. The recently built neo-Flemish Hôtel des Tours has a modern business-traveller feel despite the fact that part of it is behind an old façade, but the mezzanine rooms, which sleep two to four, are pleasantly spacious.

Hôtel de la Treille €€ *7–9 place Louise de Bettignies, tel: 03 20 55 45 46, fax: 03 20 51 51 69, <www.hoteldelatreille.fr.st>*. This pleasant modern hotel with stylish glass-fronted lobby has a great location in the heart of Vieux Lille. Bedrooms aren't huge, though staff are very helpful.

La Viennale €€ *31 rue Jean-Jacques Rousseau, tel: 03 20 51 08 02, fax: 03 20 42 17 23, <http://laviennale.free.fr>*. If you like an atmosphere that is closer to a house than a hotel, then the eccentric Viennale might be for you. Ornate salons mix original mouldings and period furniture with Oriental Buddhas and colourful silk voiles. Rooms vary from basic to the decorative: one has a wrought-iron four-poster bed; the suite has elaborate panelled bookcases; and some have complete kitchens for a longer stay. There's a garden where you can breakfast when it's fine.

LILLE MÉTROPOLE

Mercure Grand Hôtel €€ *22 avenue Jean-Baptiste Lebas, Roubaix, tel: 03 20 73 40 00, fax: 03 20 73 22 42, <www.mercure. com>.* Amid former textile company headquarters, the Grand has a striking early 20th-century facade and lobby. Bedrooms are standard but comfortable; the restaurant, despite the addition of a peculiar mezzanine, reveals touches of old grandeur in its moulded capitals and cornice.

EXCURSIONS FROM LILLE

ARRAS

Hôtel de l'Univers €€–€€€ *3–5 place de la Croix-Rouge, Arras, tel: 03 21 71 34 01, fax: 03 21 71 41 42, <www.hotel-univers-arras. com>.* Housed in an elegant 18th-century former monastery not far from the Musée des Beaux-Arts, the Univers offers old-fashioned charm with light, renovated rooms and a comfortable restaurant.

CASSEL

Châtellerie de Schoebeque €€€ *32 rue Foch, Cassel, tel: 03 28 42 42 67, fax: 03 28 42 21 86, <www.schoebeque.com>.* This 18th-century mansion was Maréchal Foch's HQ during World War I. Now totally renovated, the 15 romantic rooms vary in style from antique-filled to contemporary design, and include the 4 Saisons suite with a nook for children in an old dovecote, and two spacious 'cottages' at the end of the garden. Beauty spa and heated outdoor pool.

Hôtel Foch € *41 Grand' Place, Cassel, tel: 03 28 42 47 73, fax : 03 28 40 53 56, <www.hotel-foch.net>.* A basic but pleasant, well-tended hotel-restaurant on the picturesque main square.

ST-OMER

Ibis St-Omer € *2 rue Dupuis, St-Omer, tel: 03 21 93 11 11, fax: 03 21 88 80 20, <www.ibishotel.com>.* Well-placed hotel in the centre of town. Rooms are functional behind an old façade.

Recommended Restaurants

Lille's restaurants range from retro *estaminets* (inns) and brasseries, serving up mussels and chips, to elegant establishments specialising in the classics of French cuisine. A number of chefs are modernising traditional northern French cuisine, changing their menus according to the market but still making use of such characteristic northern ingredients and flavourings as chicory, *ginièvre*, beer, hops, *speculoos* biscuits or pungent maroilles cheese; other chefs are introducing influences from the Mediterranean and beyond. Note that dining options are limited on Sunday and Monday, when many restaurants are closed (also for all or part of August), and the best bet may be one of the brasseries around the station, on rue de Béthune or on place Rihour. Brasseries and cafés are also the best places to eat outside standard meal times or late at night.

Below is a selection of Lille's best eating places at all price levels, including some informal café-type settings and some of the city's most commendable foreign restaurants. Price guidelines are based on the average price of a three-course meal or fixed-price dinner menu for one person, including VAT and service, but not including wine. Many places also do inexpensive lunchtime menus.

€€€€	over €60
€€€	€35–60
€€	€20–35
€	up to €20

LILLE

A l'Huîtrière €€€€ *3 rue des Chats Bossus, tel: 03 20 55 43 41, <www.huitriere.fr>*. Lille's grandest restaurant has been the place to come for a special occasion for over a century. The elegant panelled dining room is located above a stunning tiled art deco fishmonger and deli. The classic fish and seafood preparations, including turbot with beer sauce and a luxurious all-shellfish menu, are beautifully realised. Superb wine list, too. Closed dinner Sun and mid-July to mid-Aug.

Alcide €€ *5 rue du Débris St-Etienne, tel: 03 20 12 06 95.* With its old-fashioned waiter service and lovely vintage interior, this brasserie, tucked down a narrow passage just off the Grand' Place, is a great place to discover regional classics like mussels, chicken *waterzoi* and *carbonnade de boeuf.* Closed dinner Sun, and mid-July to mid-Aug.

L'Arrière Pays € *47 rue Basse, tel: 03 20 13 80 07.* Convivial, inexpensive café-bistro-épicerie where you can lunch on pasta, salads and hot or cold *tartines* (open sandwiches), as well as buying grocery items to take home. Brunch on Sun. Closed 1–15 Aug.

L'Assiette du Marché €€ *61 rue de la Monnaie, tel: 03 20 06 83 61, <www.assiettedumarche.com>.* Opened in 2004 by the son of the owner of L'Huîtrière, the Assiette du Marché gives a clever contemporary edge to an elegant 18th-century *hôtel particulier*. Food is sophisticated, modern bistro cooking with an excellent-value *menu du marché*, which changes every week, and good desserts. Closed Sun.

Aux Moules €–€€ *34 rue de Béthune, tel: 03 20 57 12 46, <www.auxmoules.com>.* They do serve regional specialities and brasserie classics at this Lille institution, but the *raison d'être*, as the name suggests, is mussels, prepared *à la marinière*, *à la crème*, etc, and served in big individual saucepans accompanied by a bowl of *frites*. The 1930s' decor is a treat too, with its cracked-tile floor, red leatherette banquettes, brass coat hooks and a tile frieze of mussel fishermen.

Banyan €€€ *189 rue de Solférino, tel: 03 20 57 20 20.* Lille is home to a number of the best Thai restaurants in France, and this is many people's favourite. Refined Thai fare is served up by costumed staff in an elegant colonial setting. Closed lunch Sat and all day Sun.

Basilic Café € *10 rue du Pont-Neuf, tel: 03 28 36 91 33.* With its large, umbrella-shaded terrace, Basilic is popular with families for Sunday brunch after a visit to the market on place du Concert, and a rare place for vegetarian options. Lunchtime only (until 4pm).

Bistrot Tourangeau €€ *61 boulevard Louis XIV, tel: 03 20 52 74 64.* Not far from the Grand Palais conference centre, this attractive bistro run by brothers Hervé and Hugues Hochant focuses on the wines and specialities of the Loire valley: *boeuf à la chinonnaise*, *souris d'agneau à l'angevin* or monkfish in seaweed sauce. Closed Sun and lunch Sat. They also run the simpler Bouillon de Louis two doors away.

Brasserie André €€€ *71 rue de Béthune, tel: 03 20 54 75 51.* Its period interior and fine-weather terrace make this historic brasserie a local favourite. Quintessential brasserie fare, including steaks, fish and choucroute, as well as some more elaborate dishes, are served all day.

La Chicorée € *15 place Rihour, tel: 03 20 54 81 52.* This huge all-night brasserie is a standby for tourists by day and hungry party-goers by night, whether for a beer or onion soup, mussels or a steak in the early hours. Open 11am–4.30am, until 6am Fri and Sat.

Clément Marot €€ *16 rue de Pas, tel: 03 20 57 01 10.* One of Lille's best gastronomic secrets, where owner Clément Marot and chef François Vandeweghe cook up elegant and inventive dishes based on regional produce. Closed dinner Sun.

Le Compostelle €€ *4 rue Saint-Etienne, tel: 03 28 38 08 30, <www.lecompostelle.fr>.* This stunning Renaissance house built in 1572 was once a pilgrims' halt on the route to Santiago de Compostela in Spain. Today you can eat in the glazed-in forecourt with its ancient fountain or in one of a number of little dining rooms upstairs. Elegantly presented dishes mix fashionable cosmopolitan influences with Lillois tradition – think veal with maroilles, noisettes of lamb with beetroot, or more modern crab with lightly spiced apple and pink grapefruit.

La Coquille €€ *60 rue St-Etienne, tel: 03 20 54 29 82.* In a delightfully rustic old Flemish house with exposed brick walls and lace curtains, owner-chef Olivier Deleval does a delicious modern take on northern specialities and seasonal produce, using flavourings such as beer and chicory. He is particularly good with fish, though he also does an upmarket take on *potjevleesch* (adding foie gras to the usual chicken, rabbit and pork). Superb value. Closed Sun and 1–15 Aug.

L'Ecume des Mers €€ *10 rue de Pas, tel: 03 20 54 95 40, <www.ecume-des-mers.com>.* With its blue-and-white marine exterior and galleried dining room, this brasserie is a favourite with fish-lovers. There's a tempting display of oysters and other shellfish and a fish menu that changes daily, plus some meat dishes. Closed dinner Sun.

L'Esplanade €€€€ *84 façade de l'Espanade, tel: 03 20 06 58 58.* This restaurant, a little way out of the centre towards the Citadelle, has a growing reputation. Young chef Christophe Scherpereel is a rising talent (he previously worked at haute-cuisine temples Bernard Loiseau in Burgundy and La Tour d'Argent in Paris). Expensive à la carte but the bargain weekday lunch menu is a good way to sample Scherpereel's style. Closed Sun and lunch Sat.

Estaminet Chez La Vieille € *60 rue de Gand, tel: 03 28 36 40 06.* Under the same ownership as T'Rijsel *(see below)*, the 'old lady' plays the *estaminet* nostalgia trip to the maximum, despite it being only a few years old. With exposed bricks, old prints and photographs, advertising plaques and bric-à-brac, it's more the setting that's the draw than the variable regional fare, such as leek tart, rabbit with prunes, chicken with maroilles and boards of charcuterie and cheeses. Ice creams include curiosities such as chicory and beetroot flavours. Closed Mon, Sun and three weeks in Aug.

Estaminet de la rue Royale €€ *37 rue Royale, tel: 03 20 42 10 11.* A tiny authentic *estaminet* with zinc-topped bar and old blue-and-white china. Hot food is served only at lunchtime and Friday evening (reservation recommended), when the place soon fills up for homely, well-prepared dishes such as rabbit stew or beef with morel mushrooms. Unlike at some of its more touristy competitors, the emphasis here is on the cooking, not nostalgia. In the afternoon an eclectic crowd comes by for tea or a drink. Closed Sun.

Estaminet T'Rijsel € *25 rue de Gand, tel: 03 20 15 01 59.* This characterful *estaminet*, with candlelit tables and walls plastered with old photos and advertising plaques, is proudly *Ch'ti* and always bursting at the seams, as much for the atmosphere as the inexpensive regional food and beers on draught. Closed Mon, Sun and three weeks in Aug.

In Bocca Al Lupo €€ *1 rue des Vieux Murs, tel: 03 20 06 39 98,* *<www.in-bocca-al-lupo.com>*. Overlooking the old weavers' cottages on place aux Oignons, this Italian restaurant in Vieux Lille has a stylish yet cheery red-and-black minimalist decor. A great place to wolf down pasta or classic veal dishes. The name, which means 'in the mouth of the wolf', is an Italian expression meaning good luck. Closed Mon and dinner Tues, Wed and Sun.

Les Jardins de Serrano/La Veranda €€ *11 rue Basse or 26 rue Lepelletier, tel: 03 20 31 10 53.* The setting is the real draw here: inside in winter; outdoors in a lovely 18th-century courtyard or on the roof terrace in summer. Despite the name, the food is essentially French standards (steaks, salmon tartare, duck fillet) with some cosmopolitan touches.

Lakson €€ *21 rue du Curé St-Etienne, tel: 03 20 31 19 96.* A Swedish restaurant and deli offering a trip to the far north. The gravlax is superb, or go for exotic dishes such as smoked reindeer with Arctic berries. Closed Mon and Sun.

La Part des Anges €€ *50 rue de la Monnaie, tel: 03 20 06 44 01.* Quietly smart La Part des Anges is the wine bar interloper in the land of beer. A large choice of wines by glass or bottle can be accompanied by plates of cheese or charcuterie downstairs, with a more formal section serving hot dishes upstairs.

La Petite Cour €€ *17 rue du Curé-St-Etienne, tel: 03 20 51 52 81.* Old-fashioned dishes, such as *blanquette de veau*, salt pork with lentils, and chocolate mousse, are served in the high-ceilinged rooms of a 17th-century building with tables in a pleasant courtyard in summer. Closed Mon and Sun.

Le Pot Beaujolais €€ *26 rue de Paris, tel: 03 20 57 38 38.* This Lyonnais-style *bouchon* is a place for carnivores with its high-quality steaks, including a vast *côte de boeuf* for two, as well as other Rhône specialities, such as St-Marcellin cheese. Wines from the Beaujolais and Côtes du Rhône. Tartines, terrines and charcuterie are served all day. Closed dinner Mon, all Sun.

Le Pourquoi Pas €€ *62 rue de Gand, tel: 03 20 06 25 86.* One of the best options on the rue de Gand drag, with spaciously set tables and original cooking. Closed Sun and lunch Wed and Sat.

Le Square d'Aramis €€ *52 rue Basse, tel: 03 20 74 16 17, <www.lesquaredaramis.com>.* Trendy spot in Vieux Lille. The front room with *banquettes* and wooden tables makes for good people-watching opportunities at the corner location, while behind are a cosier space and a mezzanine with red velvet chairs and modern oil paintings. Food is a mix of the funky (lamb crumble, Thai tartare) and the regional (powerful *tarte aux maroilles*, a good *carbonnade de boeuf*).

La Terrasse des Remparts €€ *Logis de la Porte de Gand, rue de Gand, tel: 03 20 06 74 74, <www.terrassedesremparts.fr>.* The spectacular setting within one of the historic town gateways, with its bricks, terrace and glazed veranda, is draw enough, but the imaginative modern fare is pretty good too. Though there are a few regional standards on the *carte*, Mediterranean touches prevail in dishes such as lamb with thyme and coco beans or Catalan-style snails. Dinner only and Sun lunch.

Les Trois Brasseurs € *22 place de la Gare, tel: 03 20 06 46 25.* This brasserie was one of the originators of the micro-brasserie trend when it began brewing beers here on the premises in the 1980s. The beers are unfiltered and unpasteurised, while food includes mussels and *flammekueche* (onion and bacon tart).

LILLE MÉTROPOLE

L'Alimentation €–€€ *La Condition Publique, 14 place Faidherbe, Roubaix, tel: 03 28 33 48 28.* Bar at the front and a funky restaurant at the back, furnished with a hotchpotch of chairs and tables and all manner of lights dripping from the ceiling, the arty restaurant at Roubaix's Maison Folie is as original as the rest of the venue. The food is an inventive take on *terroir* (the idea that food reflects it place of origin or roots). Closed all day Mon and Sun, dinner Tues–Thur.

Auberge du Forgeron €€–€€€ *17 rue Roger Bouvry, Seclin, tel: 03 20 90 09 52, <www.aubergeduforgeron.fr>.* In this former coaching inn, young chef Philippe Bélot puts a gastronomic spin on northern specialities such as *langue Lucullus* and turbot cooked in beer. As well as the main restaurant, the auberge has a simpler bistro annexe and some pleasant bedrooms (€).

Auberge de la Garenne €€€ *17 chemin de Ghesles, Marcq-en-Barœul, tel: 03 20 46 20 20, <www.aubergegarenne.fr>.* Set amid the meadows of Lille Métropole at its most rural, this upmarket restaurant in a discreet, low modern pavilion has a garden, across which chickens occasionally amble. The menu includes French classics and elegant versions of regional dishes such as *coq à la bière*. Closed all Mon and Tues, dinner Sun.

La Grande Brasserie de l'Imperatrice Eugénie € *place de la Liberté, Roubaix, tel: 03 28 33 74 95.* Named after the Empress Eugénie, who visited the town in the 19th century, this cheerful brasserie on a colourfully painted revamped square is run by an enthusiastic young team.

La Laîterie €€€ *138 avenue de l'Hippodrome, Lambersart, tel: 03 20 92 79 73 , <www.lalaiterie.fr>.* This is the place everyone has been talking about since it was taken over in 2003 by Benoît Bernard, one of France's most hotly tipped young chefs. His cooking is an imaginative contemporary marriage of French heritage and ideas from his travels around the globe, and much of the produce is organic. Put yourself in the chef's hands with one of the tasting menus, which vary according to the produce and inspiration of the moment. Closed Mon and dinner Sun.

EXCURSIONS FROM LILLE

BOULOGNE-SUR-MER

Estaminet du Château €€ *2 rue du Château, tel: 03 21 91 49 66.* At the top end of the Haute Ville's touristy restaurant drag, here is a genuine *estaminet* – a popular local bar in one half, cheerful regional restaurant in the other – think red checked tablecloths and specialities such as herrings.

La Matelote €€€ *80 boulevard Ste-Beuve, tel: 03 21 30 17 97.* Boulogne's chic eat is a well-dressed affair in a 1930s' house facing the Nausicaa aquarium. Owner-chef Tony Estienne is known for his refined, creative cuisine. The fish is particuarly good: perhaps a combination of marinated salmon and raw oysters or roast fish with *pipérade*. Closed Sun dinner. He also owns the comfortable Hôtel de la Matelote next door (tel: 03 21 30 33 33, €€–€€€).

BUSNES

Château de Beaulieu – Marc Meurin €€€€ *rue de Lillers, tel: 03 21 68 88 88, <www.le-meurin.fr>.* Marc Meurin has moved from his restaurant in the centre of Béthune to a 17th-century château set in spacious grounds at Busnes between Calais and Lille. As well as the gastronomic restaurant, with its original yet north-infused take on grand ingredients and superlative service, there are also 20 comfortable bedrooms and suites (€€€–€€€€), and the less-expensive Jardin d'Alice (€€), an alternative modern lounge-style restaurant. Closed lunch Mon, Tues and Sat, dinner Sun.

LE CATEAU-CAMBRESIS

Hostellerie du Marché €€ *45 rue de Landrecies, tel: 03 27 84 09 32.* This rustic-styled restaurant attracts local businesses for its satisfying traditional cooking, while upstairs cosy bedrooms (€) make this the best place to stay in Le Cateau. Closed Mon and dinner Sun.

DUNKERQUE

L'Estouffade €€€ *2 quai de la Citadelle, tel: 03 28 63 92 78.* There's classic cooking and a genuinely warm welcome at this 1950s' restaurant overlooking the port. The menu is centred on, but not exclusively restricted to, fish, with such dishes as asparagus with a mousseline sauce, foie gras, delicate baby sole and brill in beer sauce. Closed Mon and dinner Sun.

INDEX